The Theology of Samuel Beckett

CALDER PUBLICATIONS
an imprint of

ALMA BOOKS LTD
3 Castle Yard
Richmond
Surrey TW10 6TF

www.calderpublications.com

First published in Great Britain by Calder Publications in 2012

Cover image © John Minihan

Printed by CreateSpace

Typeset by Tetragon

ISBN: 978-0-7145-4383-3

The Theology of
Samuel Beckett

JOHN CALDER

CALDER

*The Theology of
Samuel Beckett*

Contents

I

Beckett and God

Although the last century has in the main been a secular one, especially in countries that have for many centuries been Christian, most children have been brought up with at least an awareness of a religion, even if their parents did not go to church except perhaps for weddings, funerals and some other special occasions. Indifference to religion has been more common than declared atheism and, in spite of a few writers like Dawkins and Hitchens, there are few militant atheists, because where tolerance has been general, certainly among the educated classes, such dogmatism would have been seen as pointlessly antisocial.

My previous book, *The Philosophy of Samuel Beckett*,* went quite deeply into Beckett's thinking about God, but it did not examine in detail the progress of that thinking from childhood through his years of

---

*   John Calder, *The Philosophy of Samuel Beckett* (London: Calder Publications, 2001).

education and on to his last written works, where in essence he developed a new imaginative and literary theology of his own, one of incredible audacity and originality. The purpose of this book is to put right that omission and also to advance some thinking of my own on the same subject.

Studies of Beckett's work continue to multiply, but in general certain aspects of his thinking are avoided, especially by academics, who tend to go into quite obscure, and in my view unimportant, supposed influences on him, often bringing in names that he would have known, or books he might have glanced at, but without much effect on his own thinking and writing. There are various reasons for this, especially among academics, who are always aware that the advancement of their careers could be affected if they introduce into their teaching opinions against a current orthodoxy or deeply felt prejudice. This is certainly true in the United States, where I have often been told, "If I taught *that* I would lose my job and never get another." This applies particularly to references to God and to religion in general. At a conference in York University in June 2011, after listening to many lectures, all of them carefully read from prepared texts, I commented that three potent influences on Samuel Beckett's work had not been mentioned once, namely Shakespeare, Milton and God. In a subsequent lecture tour of my own around Ireland, I concentrated largely on those three names, as well as on certain philosophers that I will come to later. I pointed out that there is not a single character in Beckett's novels or plays who is not a religious believer, that theological ideas, discussions and speculations abound everywhere in his work and that the author found the Christian religion in particular a rich source for his imagination and a background to his writing.

What many people find difficult to accept is the blurred line between faith and general interest, especially where the latter is present in someone deeply knowledgeable on the subject and where that knowledge was established early in life. The commonly held notion that loss of faith is followed by loss of interest is just not true. It applies mainly to those who think of God in the narrow terms of a personal and conscious being, who when rejected ceases to exist at all. For centuries, even going back to the Gnostics in the early Christian era and to such older religions as Hinduism and Zoroastrianism, with which the Gnostics had much in common, deeper thinkers have had a very different idea of the possibility of the existence of a supreme being, still undefined, that might be called God or Nature or some presence beyond infinity, itself indefinable.

In any examination of Samuel Beckett's work, it is necessary to posit the presence of a dualism that applies equally to the man and his work. In so far as Manichaeism is concerned there is much to say, not only of his direct fascination with one of the most interesting of the so-called heresies, but in the recurrence of opposing twosomes throughout his writing. His characters tend to come in pairs, Vladimir and Estragon, Pozzo and Lucky, Hamm and Clov, Nagg and Nell, Mercier and Camier, Molloy and Moran and so on, each tending to be the logical opposite of the other. Manichaeism contrasts good and evil like day and night and is based upon a perception of the world that, while admitting that God might have created it, also recognizes that he did so very ineptly, and probably did not quite realize what he had done. He might therefore have appointed a deputy to run things for him, which to the Manichaeans could well have been the Devil. The balance of good and evil in the world always indicated the heavier weight of the latter. This comes out in various austere sects, most notably the Cathars of Provence, who appeared in the eleventh century and were brutally massacred by the Catholic Church two hundred years later. *Krapp's Last Tape* is not only Beckett's most autobiographical play, but it is also carefully structured on Manichaean principles with each event, object or reference either white or black, the two balanced as equally as possible. It represents, as it is described in one speech by the protagonist, "the vision at last",* the moment when Beckett himself realized that his future as a writer lay not in avoiding his dark view of humanity and the world, but in accepting it and making it the spur to push his writing forward.

---

* Samuel Beckett, *The Complete Dramatic Works* (London: Faber & Faber, 2006), p. 220.

Beckett's dualism comes out nowhere better than in his thinking about religion. Much of his talent as a humorist went into mocking or making fun of the absurdities of many conventional beliefs, but he cannot be described as a believer, a non-believer, an atheist or even an agnostic. He disbelieved with a large doubt or disbelieved reluctantly or, more accurately, he kept the belief and disbelief poised in his mind, always unresolved, while he went on consciously speculating about the nature and the existence of God.

Of course, everything starts in childhood. Beckett's father was a large man, fond of walking and the open air, a successful businessman who had built his own house in Foxrock, a pleasant suburb of South Dublin, as well as much else in the area, near to a racecourse and not far from the sea. He was a fairly regular, if not a particularly devout churchgoer, probably as much from social obligation and conformity as from any innate piety, but he was a prominent member of the Anglo-Irish community, and of the Protestant Church of Ireland, like most of his class. Samuel Beckett's mother, on the other hand, was an extremely pious and observant Quaker. The earliest photograph of the young Samuel shows him kneeling at his mother's knee, being taught his prayers, which he still remembered in old age. He always had a vivid memory of such moments and would recall them in his work, to such an extent that a reasonable biography could be constructed from his prose fiction alone, which is dotted with first- or third-person self-portraits. Religion was pumped into him as a child and at primary school, and he was then sent to the elitist college for affluent Irish Protestants at Enniskillen in the North, Portora Royal High School. This, in those days, was a stern Calvinist institution, where the tenets of the strictest and most intolerant branch of Protestantism were further inculcated into him. In the first section of Lucky's speech in *Waiting for Godot*, some of those tenets are resurrected, although in a very incoherent form. What is remembered there is the Calvinist doctrine of predestination, which suggests that because God is all powerful and all knowing he must be aware of everything in advance, and therefore sinners are condemned to hell even centuries before their birth. This concept does not exist among Catholics with their belief in repentance and a more merciful God. It undoubtedly had an importance in the thinking of the teenage Beckett, and must have worried him for years. All his life he was preoccupied by injustice, and a doctrine that could condemn a person to damnation even before he or she had come into existence must have played a large part in his loss of a strict faith, which undoubtedly did happen, either at the school or later when he went on to Trinity College in Dublin. As a student and soon an admiring follower of Shakespeare, the relevance of predestination to the bard's evil or tragically troubled characters must have occurred to him. Iago and Richard III, Macbeth and even Hamlet could be the objects of the Calvinist

God's wrath. But it was at Trinity that he made the great discovery that was to influence his entire future, although only after he returned there as a lecturer.

In the library of Trinity College, probably by accident while browsing among the bookshelves, he came across a name that was almost certainly unknown to anyone else there. Philosophy was one of Beckett's minor subjects, and it would have been on the shelves devoted to it that he came across the *Ethica* of Arnold Geulincx (1624–69), a long-forgotten seventeenth-century Flemish or Dutch theologian, a follower of Descartes, who nevertheless went far beyond Cartesianism in his enquiries into the human condition and the existence of God. Today labelled an occasionalist, Arnold Geulincx found interesting metaphors for the relationship between man and God, which Beckett would later record in his notes. Occasionalism is the belief that God is the cause of all events and that our perception of causation – that is, of one event happening as a result of another – is an illusion. But at the same time, like followers of Hinduism, who believe their supreme being to be an enormous distance away and instead attribute divine intervention in human affairs to avatars, Geulincx thought deeply about infinity and the vastness of space around us and far out into the universe. The seventeenth century was a time when scientific knowledge was growing fast through the observations of such searchers for meaning as Galileo, and such learning continued to grow in spite of the opposition of Christian Churches and especially the Inquisition. Trinity at the time of Beckett's presence there was still emerging intellectually from the Dark Ages with its burden of medieval scholastic philosophy, but free thought was possible and certainly taught, and the Protestant ethic was far freer than the Catholic, soon to fall under the authoritarianism of the De Valera era from 1922 onwards.

Although less well known than his contemporary Malebranche, also labelled an occasionalist, Geulincx was in many ways more radical and certainly more aware of time and space than any other thinker of his time. He saw God as being so far away that he was not necessarily aware of our very presence, a remote group of intelligent beings on a far-away planet, one of so many billions (as we know today). For that reason we should be aware of our near irrelevance, our almost nonexistence, and we should accept the humility which is our due. Geulincx's key quotation which Beckett often used is "*Ubi nihil vales ibi nihil velis*", which says that where one is worth nothing one should act accordingly and be totally humble, that is, nothing. The shortness of life, which was to become the keynote in Beckett's world view, probably originates in his discovery of Geulincx, along with the conviction that there is nothing to be done about it. These were to become the words that opened Beckett's best-known play, almost certainly the major play of the twentieth century, *Waiting for Godot*: "*Rien à faire*", or,

"Nothing to be done". One lives for a short time and then one dies. It is summarized in Pozzo's departing speech in *Godot* and echoed in a spasm of agony a few minutes later by Vladimir, who almost succumbs to despair, then pulls himself back from the brink at the last moment. The vast expanse of time and space, the shortness of life: those two phrases sum up the philosophies of both Geulincx and Beckett. But what a world of literature the latter was to make out of it!

It was said of nineteenth-century scientists and thinkers such as Darwin and Huxley that they had put God farther away. The realization of the great distances between galaxies and of how much can be contained inside a single atom, and the growth of scientific knowledge in general, has made the old fundamental beliefs impossible, except for those who are unwilling to face the world of logic and proven evidence. When Geulincx put God so far away that he doubted if such a presence could even be aware of our existence, the old general confidence that another world awaited us after death no longer held much credence. This too must have gone through Beckett's thinking during the time that he studied philosophy at Trinity under Arthur Aston Luce, although he was mainly studying French and Italian, and Dante in particular had a major impact on him. In later life not only could he quote whole pages from *The Divine Comedy*, but many images from the great Italian poet would surface in his own writing. For instance, the poem 'dread nay' contains the fearful image from the ninth circle of hell of Satan endlessly chewing a great sinner with each of his three giant heads. The poem's title indicates Beckett's own loss of faith in the existence of Dante's Inferno, but the image is there. Nevertheless hell comes up in his work many times, including even the very late writings, where his theological speculations had returned in a daring new form. In another poem, 'Malacoda', Beckett imagined his dead father being carried off to another world, but also indicates his scepticism.* Disbelief was always there, but in a dualistic and questioning form.

In his imagination at least, from early Calvinism through Dante and on to his own work, hell is frequently present. He once investigated Purgatory when doing research for James Joyce in the Thirties, although he was already well acquainted with Dante's *Purgatorio*, which is where he found his alter ego, Belacqua, who moves through Beckett's early fictions, most notably *More Pricks than Kicks*. Belacqua's vice is laziness and the desire only to sit and contemplate, which Beckett attributed to himself, as perhaps his parents did because of his reluctance after his studies to take a normal job and earn a conventional living. There is little mention of heaven in Beckett's writing, perhaps because it is so little depicted or described in literature, painting or the other arts. A form of afterlife is invented by Beckett in his plays and occasionally in his fiction, *The*

---

* For 'Malacoda' and 'dread nay' see Samuel Beckett, *Selected Poems 1930–1989* (London: Faber & Faber, 2009), pp. 30, 66–67.

Unnamable in particular. It is always closely related to the life just lived. The inference is that an afterlife is not for long, and this may arise from his knowledge that the mind can continue working for some time after the heart has stopped. Beckett may have been aware of a grisly experiment, widely reported in the French press early in the century, in which two murderers agreed that after guillotining their heads would be put on cushions and they would be interrogated for as long as their eyelids could respond by blinking to indicate 'Yes' or 'No'. The interrogation went on for several minutes and this could have had a very strong impression on the writer had he come across it, which, if he had, would most likely have been after the war. He was then trying to return to normal life after years of hiding in the Vaucluse mountains. He had spent most of the war there, having earlier escaped the Gestapo who were looking for him for his activities with the Resistance in Paris after the Occupation had taken place.

Disembodied voices in the air are present in *Waiting for Godot*, at least in the imagination of the two tramps, and heads surmounting jars occur in *Play* and elsewhere. The sight is of course common in France, where signs outside restaurants often depict a chef's head with the menu hanging around his neck. But there is no indication in Beckett that such post-death consciousness and ability to think are for ever or even for long. Among his many dualisms hell has an existence, heaven not. Short-term memory continuing after death might be construed as Purgatory. There are also ghosts in some of the plays and they too represent a form of afterlife.

The logical assumption from Geulincx to Beckett is that while some form of deity might exist, it is not necessarily a conscious one. And such a deity is not necessarily aware of any human presence, nor does there have to be any significant afterlife except in imagination. The whole system of belief in a divine judgement and afterlife in monotheism becomes no more credible than in the old pagan afterworld beyond the Styx. Beckett even makes a jocular reference to this when he refers in the play *Embers* to "small chat to the babbling of Lethe about the good old days when we wished we were dead".*

One does not have to question Christian or other monotheistic beliefs for long before realizing that a firm faith is based less on worship and love of a God, who presumably loves us back, than on a concern for our own ultimate fate and rewarding afterlife. What is the point of loving a God who has no interest in us and if our existence ends with our lives? Devotion and belief are really only self-love. Beckett realized this very clearly, but the emotional pull of childhood belief never entirely left him, which is why he was able to say in later life, "You never know." It is almost impossible for anyone brought up with a strong conventional

---

* Beckett, *The Complete Dramatic Works*, p. 256.

belief ever to get it wholly out of their mind. Everyday remarks on meeting or parting reflect this, such as "God bless", "God willing" or "God go with you", which are automatic statements of which the speaker is hardly conscious. Many with a Roman Catholic background who have ceased practising still make the sign of the cross at the passing of a hearse or some such event that brings an instinctive religious response. The dualism of a nostalgic belief and the rejection of belief is a principle key to all of Beckett's work, and also the rich source from which he was able to produce a literature that was both comic and tragic and has come to be recognized as the most significant writing of its time, in terms of both its imaginative invention and its portrayal of the reality of the existence in which we are forced to pass our lives – long or short, endurable or not. No other writer comes near Beckett in describing that reality.

But he went much further than using the religion he knew and grew up with as background material for his work. Like Dante and Milton he invented a shadow world from the one we inhabit, first as a satirist pulling the strings from the scriptures to form new connections, and later to create a new theology, which is daring and logical and based on a personal philosophy that I have already described in essence in my earlier book, *The Philosophy of Samuel Beckett.*

2

A Passion for Painting

One aspect of Samuel Beckett's preoccupations that, until now – over twenty years after his death – has been little examined, is his deep interest in the visual arts, something that goes back to his student days and which also offers an insight into his work, from at least *Waiting for Godot* until *Ill Seen Ill Said*. That he had many artist friends is well known, but the publication of his collected correspondence, and in particular his letters to his close friend Thomas MacGreevy, has revealed how intense his interest in painting, and to a lesser extent sculpture, was. As a student at Trinity he was a frequent visitor to the National Gallery of Ireland, which stood very near his father's old Dublin office at 6 Clare Street, and even closer to the university.

In 2006 the gallery published an illustrated catalogue containing numerous essays to accompany an exhibition devoted to Beckett's interest in paintings and the works that he particularly admired.* It is interesting to note that while many of these were by personal friends such as Jack Yeats, this was not necessarily always the case. During the Thirties, when not in Paris, Beckett spent time in Germany and aside from discovering much German literature, mainly of the Romantic period, he spent most of his time in art galleries. Many of the paintings that he saw then and earlier played a part in his later dramatic career, as for instance the painting by Caspar David Friedrich of *Two Men Contemplating the Moon*, which is generally believed to have inspired the closing scenes of *Godot*, when the moon rises and attracts the attention of the two tramps.

A large part of any public art gallery is devoted to religious paintings and these must have taken up a good deal of Beckett's viewing time. When in 1931 the National Gallery in Dublin acquired the *Pietà* by Perugino, Beckett paid it many visits, complaining that it was badly hung and partially obscured by a barrier of shining glass. It depicts the stretched-out body of Jesus after he is brought down from the cross. His face is calm and there are no visible signs of injury on the body, which partly lies across his mother's knees with other saintly figures watching, all with haloes, one of them being Mary Magdalene. I mention elsewhere in this book that Beckett's interest in the Virgin Mary

* Fionnuala Croke, ed., *Samuel Beckett: A Passion for Paintings* (Dublin: National Gallery of Ireland, 2006).

(apart from Magdalene) may not be totally unconnected with the similarity of the name to that of his
mother, May, which, along with its anagram, Amy, is
given to a character in the play *Footfalls*. The Virgin
Mary I shall come to later when discussing *Ill Seen Ill
Said*, but the Perugino painting may well have struck
a chord with Beckett, reminding him of his childhood
and of the great love his mother had for him, as well
as her anxiety over his disappearing religious beliefs.
It certainly gave her great pain when the Dublin newspapers called him "the atheist from Paris" during the
Gogarty trial,* when in the witness box he affirmed
the absence of any particular faith. Guilt at causing
her suffering must have continued through his relationship with her and certainly, when she was dying and
there was only him to care for her, he may well have
remembered the Perugino and compared his mother's
distress at his agnosticism with that of the Virgin Mary
for the dead Jesus. One might go further and suggest
that all Beckett's women, certainly the old woman
in *Ill Seen* and perhaps even Winnie in *Happy Days*
and the nameless speaker in *Rockaby*, are really all
based on his mother, to whom over the years he had
caused much distress by moving to Paris, adopting a

---

* A lawsuit was brought against the Irish author Oliver St John
Gogarty over his novel *As I Was Going Down Sackville Street*
(1937), which, it was claimed, contained libellous passages against
Harry Sinclair, a Jewish art dealer, and his dead brother William.
Beckett, who was related by marriage to the brothers, appeared
as a witness for the prosecution.

very different lifestyle and being the failure that she so closely believed him to be.

The catalogue put out by the National Gallery of Ireland emphasizes not only Samuel Beckett's great interest in and understanding of painting of all periods, but his understanding of the creative and intellectual forces that went into the art itself. He also had a photographic memory that enabled him to recall the details as well as the composition of paintings that had made an impression on him. *The Assumption of St Mary Magdalene* by Silvestro dei Gherarducci in one gallery would seem to have been the visual inspiration for the figure of May in *Footfalls*. The National Gallery catalogue juxtaposes Billie Whitelaw playing the part with the altarpiece painting. The two figures are in exactly the same position, arms crossed, looking upwards. It was not so unusual in early Christian times for people to believe that bodies could be carried up to heaven instead of dying on the earth, and I will refer to this later. Beckett's interest in religious art was in the painting itself rather than the subject, but many of the images remained indelibly lodged in his mind and are used by him as references in the prose and in the stage pictures in the plays. We know that he had musical as well as literary abilities and, given his great interest in painting, it is surprising that he never, as far we know, engaged in painting itself.

3

Religion and Literature

Genius can be defined, but not until a work of genius has been created by someone who has it, and it is often not recognized among many contemporaries, remaining controversial until late in the genius's career. Even when early work has been recognized as highly talented and interesting, the later output of a literary genius often fails for a while to convince those who come to it, even if they recognize the importance of what was done in the past. This was the case with Beethoven, the musical genius who most closely resembled Beckett. The former's late work was at first considered by many of his admirers to be a sign of growing dementia and it took time for them to find their way into a new form of sound that had not previously existed in music.

As with Beethoven, Beckett's work falls into three definable periods or styles: an early one, largely reminiscent of a predecessor (Mozart in the case of Beethoven and Joyce with Beckett), a second, highly original and different, but open to enjoyment and appreciation by those already convinced, and a third that goes into a world of art where no one had ventured before. The quartets of Beethoven's late period produced totally new sounds, while the late piano sonatas also contained innovations that were new to listeners and performers. Beckett's late period can be considered as beginning with the novella *How It Is*, published in 1961, which leads the way into a period of barely concealed despair, a view of the world as a savage place of pain and suffering, depicted in a series of reflective shorter works that echo the thoughts that were wending their way through the author's mind, mainly as he sat at his desk at Ussy – "in the Marne mud", as he so often put it. Otherwise he was in Paris to keep appointments or see friends or, which was to become his greatest escape, when he involved himself in rehearsals of his plays in Paris or London, and shortly after in Germany.

Here too is a dualism. The war was over, but horrors still multiplied around the world. Colonial wars continued, and in France the demand for independence of Algerian nationalists dominated everyday life. An Italian film, *Mondo cane*, had a considerable effect on Beckett, through its depiction of random cruelties, largely in Africa, filmed by an Italian crew who may often have provoked or initiated the events in order to film them. Beckett was unable to read or hear about cruelty without suffering himself, and such was his imagination that his agony must have been extreme. During his lifetime he had had to endure much physical pain, but he always dismissed it as nothing compared to spiritual pain, which was the mental anguish that had first afflicted him in his early manhood, when escaping from his despairing parents who could not understand their work-shy son who wanted only to write books that evidently no one wanted to read. They finally gave him a small allowance, much of which must have gone on psychiatric counselling as he tried to understand himself. If a genius is fortunate enough to find himself in a congenial group of like-minded individuals, whatever his circumstances, he can be comfortable mentally, but a freethinking intellectual immured in a business world of Irish Protestant ethics can only escape with great difficulty. When he landed in Paris he was able to find such a sympathetic milieu and in spite of great poverty he was comfortable there. Not surprisingly, when the war intervened, it was in Paris that he decided to stay and when his friends joined the Resistance against the occupying Germans, it was only natural that he should do the same, mainly out of loyalty, though his travels in Germany during the Thirties had given him a good enough idea of what Nazism was about.

Although it was a good time for him in many ways, his pre-war Paris days were not very fruitful where his work was concerned. He produced some poetry, some not his best, and his monograph on Proust, and much of his time was spent doing translations of French verse and surrealist work for little Paris magazines, of which *transition* was the most notable, then serializing Joyce's still uncompleted and not-yet-titled *Finnegans Wake*. But Beckett was living in a community of kindred spirits, where the little necessities of life were shared, along with ideas, and he was in the boiling centre of the furnace of modern art, surrealism and the many other aspects of modernism that were producing new painting, literature and music, as well as innovation in drama and the other performing arts, all of which made Paris the centre of an expanding European culture before Nazism and the war closed everything down.

It is not hard to see why Beckett, who was paying a brief visit to Dublin to see his family in September 1939, rushed back to Paris to be with his friends when war broke out. The dullness and parochialism of Éamon De Valera's Ireland – priest-ridden and philistine – where he knew that he was personally not accepted, had no allure compared to the intellectual excitement of Paris and his daily immersion in the arts. When the German invasion came, France, which remembered only too well the senseless slaughter of the First World War, quickly collapsed, outmanoeuvred by German military strategists who had brought warfare into a new age, whereas the French were still thinking in terms of the trench combat of a generation earlier.

When the occupation of Paris arrived, many fled into the countryside, including at first Samuel Beckett, now accompanied by Suzanne Deschevaux-Dumesnil, who had taken care of him after he was knifed by a demented *clochard* in the street, but they returned when things calmed down. When his friends joined a group in the Resistance to help the Allies clandestinely, so did he, and when they were betrayed and mostly arrested, he was fortunate enough to be warned in time to escape Paris. Sheltered at one point outside Paris by Nathalie Sarraute and her husband, he had to share an attic room with her old father, also in hiding because he and Sarraute were Jewish, whereas her husband was not. Occupying this enclosed space with an old dying man became the inspirational origin of a major novel, *Malone Dies*, not written until more than ten years later.

Beckett's war was a time of regrouping. He had seen the rise of Nazism in Germany, but at the time had immersed himself in German culture, not only literature and music, but painting as well. He had translated many of the French surrealist poets and others as well, including German. His friendship with graphic artists had put him firmly into the Parisian art scene, and of course his close connection with James Joyce was also contributing to his creative literary powers. Now that much of his personal literary correspondence has been published, we also know that he continued to write and receive letters from old Irish friends, most notably Thomas MacGreevy, later the keeper of the National Gallery of Ireland. MacGreevy was an intimate friend to whom Beckett felt he could confide his spiritual suffering involving both his health and his work and the difficulty he had in finding just what it was he wanted to express and how to express it. Although his thoughts about the religion that he had at that point left behind were undoubtedly muted, they were probably still there in essence. Politics rather than religion would have been the talking point among Beckett's friends in Paris in the years preceding the war, but once Beckett was largely alone again, having gone into hiding with Suzanne at Roussillon after leaving Paris for good, there was time again for speculation about the religion that had played such a large part in his upbringing.

If one considers *Waiting for Godot* as being, at least in part, a fairly true representation of the conversations that Beckett had with his friend Henri Hayden (who in the play is Estragon) during his years of hiding in the Vaucluse during the war, and of his private thoughts at the time, then religious speculation – bringing up contradictions in the New Testament and other literary memories from Dante, Shakespeare and elsewhere – plays a part. His writing at the time was centred on *Watt*, the philosophical novel that follows *Murphy* and that, although avoiding direct religious reference, still has many episodes that bring up parallels with biblical ones, some of which are detailed in *The Philosophy of Samuel Beckett*.

Beckett was of course busy during his time at Roussillon. He had to earn some money and he did it by working for two local farmers, one a wine grower called Bonnelly who, as Beckett says, "made good wine". Beckett's father did manage to get some money sent to him through a Vichy area bank, which must have been both complicated and dangerous. In the evenings he worked on *Watt*. It was only when the Germans were seen to be coming towards the village, which is situated on a hilltop, that Beckett and Hayden, a Dutch painter, had to go into hiding (Hayden for being Jewish), which is of course the background situation of *Waiting for Godot*. But out of that menace, and the servile French subjugation to the occupying Germans, and much else in the play that I have described elsewhere, Beckett was to make much, which must have been growing in his mind until after 1947, when his two years of intense creativity began. In the novel *Molloy*, another project of the "siege years", the view from the top of the hill in Roussillon is described with A and C visible on the flat ground below, but miles away, seen to be approaching each other or separating. As it is clear that these are Abel and Cain, it is an early example of Beckett playing God, observing everything from a great height, but it can also be seen as the evil Nazi presence (Cain) and the enslaved but virtuous French (Abel). Although *Molloy* is clearly set in an Irish landscape, there are sometimes descriptions that suggest Roussillon and the Vaucluse. And there is a clear parallel in Moran's journey to find Molloy in the novel. In any case, once Beckett had achieved worldwide recognition, landscapes had little importance. It is what is universal and applicable to all humanity in Beckett's work that gives it its universality and a total relevance to all who come to it.

The two years spent in Roussillon were a time of reflection and of the maturing in Beckett's mind of everything that had happened to him since leaving Portora, and that he had learnt in his travels in England, France and Germany, including the psychological problems of deciding who he was, what he wanted to write and what he believed in. Doubt shrouded his mind, but his genius, not yet totally formed, drove him on. He had learnt how to relax with congenial company and to put his problems temporarily out of his mind. Although shy with women, he had normal desires, and it was usually strong and intellectually ambitious women who took the initiative where sex was concerned. His writings on sexuality are sometimes caustic, always funny, never really erotic. His self-portraits in the writings that followed the war are always self-denigratory, showing himself as others saw him, primarily his self-satisfied parents, later as the lower specimens of humanity that he saw sleeping under bridges or begging in the streets on whom he modelled Molloy, while at the same time showing how rich Molloy's mind could be.

Whereas the first fictions, the juvenile novel *Dream of Fair to Middling Women* (published posthumously, which many think was a mistake on the part of his executors) and *More Pricks Than Kicks*, using much of the same material as the first volume, are largely autobiographical, depicting the author in his student days at Trinity, the two works that followed, *Murphy* and *Watt*, are really philosophical investigations turned into narratives. Thereafter he uses metaphor in his novels and shorter prose pieces, while the plays, on which his worldwide success and reputation largely depend, are slices of life, naturalistic except where visual innovations are introduced, often with a biblical or other literary reference behind them.

This is particularly true of *Endgame*, based on the story of the Flood and Noah's Ark, but world disasters are common, such as in the short story 'Lessness', where a calamity has overtaken a tribe or a group of tribes that "will curse God again as in the blessed days".* The constant references to God, certainly not to a benevolent one, openly or partially hidden in both the prose works and the plays, are not evidence of any firm belief in Beckett's thinking, but a useful reference taken from all the material in his biblical knowledge and the nostalgic and emotional background that he could introduce into his work. It is part of the dualism earlier described.

Where this dualism is most complex is in the 'trilogy' (the novels *Molloy*, *Malone Dies* and *The Unnamable*), to which much reference is made in my earlier book, *The Philosophy of Samuel Beckett*. The New Testament seems to run through the three works, in particular

---

* Samuel Beckett, *Texts for Nothing and Other Shorter Prose 1950–1976* (London: Faber & Faber, 2010), p. 129.

where the announcement to Mary that she will bring forth a child and what follows is concerned, but the metaphors are difficult to follow, often ambiguous, and revealed as much by the names that Beckett gives to his characters as by the events described. What is most telling is the monologue of Moran in the second part of *Molloy*, where the illogical and obviously impossible or inconceivable tenets of Christianity are brought out in comic relief, some based on the more ridiculous debates of medieval Christianity. These are featured in the questions that Moran thinks up when lost in the desert, and buried among the stupidest are thought-provoking real questions such as: "What was God doing with himself before the creation?"* This is perhaps the most difficult question that can be asked of a devotee of any faith. Now that we are aware of the immensity of time past – never mind the infinity of time ahead of us – it is impossible for any thinking person not to realize that the recorded or imagined history of the human race must be totally irrelevant in the time that life has existed on this planet, which is after all only one out of an immense number of others, perhaps of an infinity of others. It has recently been calculated that the human chromosome separated from that of the higher apes about fifty-five million years ago. Compare that to the ten thousand years or so that religious belief of some form has existed to explain our world to human

---

* Samuel Beckett, *Molloy* (London: Faber & Faber, 2009), p. 175.

intelligence, and our mythological histories as known from Genesis, Egyptian, Babylonian or Oriental writing becomes insignificant. Beckett was well aware of this and Moran's question is the most basic one that any religious thinker can ask him or herself. The ability to think logically took an immense amount of time to develop, and the capacity to speculate intelligently about the nature and existence of all things took even longer. Only childhood indoctrination can keep traditional religious belief alive, and that must be backed up by dogma and the fear that lies behind all unwillingness to question what we are told by organized religion and pious mentors.

But in our modern age, except in the more fundamentalist religions – and they are increasingly inclined towards violence and extremism to maintain a firm belief – atheism and agnosticism are spreading. Scientific knowledge, made ever more urgent by the need for ever faster medical advances as people want to live longer, is gradually winning the day, though it will take longer in some parts of the world then in others.

In addition, religion always has a political element to its existence and to the way it functions, whatever the leadership of any country or any society might be, kingship, tribal leader or elected ruler; there is always a need for religious support. The Slovenian philosopher Slavoj Žižek points out that the reason the priesthood in antiquity had a privileged ascendancy, close to the kings of the day (he is referring in particular to early Greek civilization), is that, just as every species tends to devour the species immediately below its own, the function of the priesthood was to protect the kings and nobles from being eaten by the gods who ruled above them. This entailed sacrificing animals and if necessary some humans to whatever gods were believed to be all powerful in order to appease them. So, for instance, Iphigenia had to be sacrificed to enable the ships to sail for Troy and, in Genesis, Abraham was ordered to sacrifice his son Isaac, just to show his obedience. The priesthood in the first case, and the prophet in the second, were simply carrying out the will of the gods or God.

Throughout history religion is the tool of the ruler and the priests are the go-betweens to the deity, interpreting the divine wishes and commands and often carrying out the executions and punishments. This has always been the case from antiquity down through the Inquisition, and in the present day it continues in the small penances given by Catholic priests to sinners after confession. Ecclesiastics bless armies before going to war, always with the assumption that the deity is on their side, sometimes to persuade him. Only the gradual acquisition of historical and scientific knowledge can slowly subvert this belief in supernaturally imposed pressure on human behaviour, much of it highly antisocial if not positively evil, as most fanaticism essentially becomes. In our time we have seen the element of sacrifice, often treated as a duty, becoming self-sacrifice, usually with the promise of some reward in the next world.

Religious leaders, in order to convince their adherents, usually take up a position against any scientific discovery that conflicts with the tenets and writings of organized religion. The power of childhood teaching is so strong that only a small minority can be counted on to think independently and weigh up clear scientific evidence against dogma imposed by authority, often with the full weight of local law behind it.

The United States is a large, powerful and diverse society, consisting of mixed, largely ghettoized populations, and it is still largely fundamentalist in its mass thinking, holding firmly on to a religious history that goes back less than eight thousand years, during which a literacy developed that was able to record some events, much mythology and even more imaginative invention. The history that is taught in the US tends to ignore the wiping out of the population of an entire continent, the native American Indians, the development and retention of a massive and brutal slave trade, and other anti-humane events that shame American history. But every nation has similar brutalities in its recent past, some of them quite recent, and with the twentieth century now behind us – of which so much was hoped and expected in 1900 – it can be seen that nothing changed in essence in spite of all the intellectual and scientific advances where human governance and behaviour were concerned, nor is it likely to change for the better in the future: whole populations struggle to live and exist as their numbers increase and their viable environment shrinks.

As new nations emerge to surpass those that previously dominated the planet, it becomes clear that even when the intentions are basically benevolent, the necessity of dealing with insurmountable problems, many of them created by a human nature that refuses to control its ever-increasing growth, suffering, cruelty, corruption and tyranny, will always be there and that the continuance of a civilized existence, except for a few, cannot be expected.

The work of Samuel Beckett is not unique to its own immediate historical context, but remains so rich in its understanding of an existence that holds out hope neither for a return to what was less bad nor for an advance to something even marginally better that one can only admire the courage of his thinking and his grasp of reality. Man is basically a pack animal, tribal and cruel, loyal on the whole to his pack, capable on occasion of kindness, compassion and generosity, but that does not apply to everyone, and not often.

Man's main tragedy is the shortness of his life – too short to give him enough time, even if he lives beyond the average to understand his destiny – amid the hazard of birth, his birthplace and time, and all the circumstances, economic, physical and historical, that affect him, as well as the genetic circumstances of his heredity. Some are born to be creative, and because creativity overwhelms the whole personality if it is strong enough, that person may well come to a certain contentment with his or her existence. That person will be able to appreciate his ability to work and to lose himself totally in the act of creation, which, as I have pointed out previously, puts him or her into the company of the human conception of God: a creator. Of course, for those who achieve a lifestyle that offers a reasonable physical comfort with an existence based on habit, much the same can be said. But of course, it is not for ever. What is missed for most is the sense of spirituality or aesthetics, which is a human trait, not a godly one. Beckett understood this very well, largely through his study of Geulincx, where the key element in his highly unorthodox Christian thinking is the need for total humility at our contemplation of a God who is so far away that he probably does not even know we exist. One thing that Beckett did realize – and it comes up in his work over and over again – is that our planet is filled with almost indescribable horrors and that if there is a conscious God, he is indifferent to them and does nothing to prevent or stop them. At times, as with Baudelaire, God is simply described as an object for hatred, perhaps even as being the source of all suffering. This puts him back into the thinking of the Gnostics, and to a certain extent of the Manichaeans, who fascinated Beckett enough for him to base a whole play on the interplay of darkness and light, *Krapp's Last Tape* – in many ways his most autobiographical work.

His strict Protestant faith long gone by the time he was becoming a creative writer, the search for meaning and of the nature of what might have started the beginnings of creation – assuming that there was a beginning – continued throughout his life, although divine speculation was often put temporarily aside to examine purely human aspects of our existence and behaviour. Beckett was himself a true prototype of the modern outsider who, coming from an extremely conventional bourgeois family, was unable to live the life that was expected of him, with all its hypocrisies, blindness to what it is uncomfortable to see, let alone notice, and daily habits and civilities. But much of his work, especially prior to 1947, when his great middle period began, deals with that life, describing it accurately, as in his play *Eleutheria*, where he depicts himself as Victor Krap, a total outsider. Similar outbursts also featured in the trilogy and *First Love*, written in or just before 1947 when, believing he had only a short time to live because of a tumour in his cheek, he plunged into the two years of concentrated work on which his literary reputation with the general public largely depends. Suffering – his own and that of the world, unheeded by any God in whom he could believe, and ignored by the social grouping in which he grew up – is the main preoccupation of the work of that period. This is also true of what follows, but he continually turned the focus to bring new creative ideas and concepts into his writing. Much of it has still not received the attention it deserves.

Samuel Beckett's self-portrait, as described in the immediate post-war writings, is to a great extent the picture of himself that his despairing parents had before they died and he had his first success. That self-portrait was exaggerated and enlarged by his depiction in the short stories of a large household full of unfriendly relatives, especially in 'The Expelled'. The self-portrait always, or nearly always, depicts him as homeless, wandering from one place to another, usually in one of the many ruined landscapes that are so minutely described in the short texts that came out either individually or in small collections from 1958 onwards. The world is described, as we so often know parts of it to be, after a natural disaster, famine, drought, earthquake or a civil or tribal war, leaving behind dead or mangled bodies, still just alive and suffering terribly. Beckett read the newspapers and such events, in a world with no conscious God ever responding to the many prayers that were no doubt being offered by the believing religious multitudes so infected, always had a strong emotional effect on him, as if the pain were his own.

The Beckett landscape on this planet is so bleak, sometimes seen from above as by a bird, sometimes from a scene of deprivation or as a burst of useless activity as in the short story 'The Lost Ones', but also as a moving mind travelling through space that is enclosed inside a comet. So are we all, looked at by an external eye, travelling throughout the universe on our single planet, each an insignificant little presence, moving through an unimaginable immensity. His study of Geulincx's *Ethica* certainly contributed to his combining of science and speculative theocracy, either buried in fictional concepts of some suffering existence, human or animal, that can be found in so much of his work after the 1950s. This reaches a climax in the very late works that I shall come to in a later chapter.

Pity, unfortunately, does nothing to overcome the maladies of the world and the lack of divine intervention, always in conflict with Beckett's childhood-instilled beliefs, when added to the unnecessary but unstoppable growth of human cruelty, could only have had a profound effect on a mind as sensitive, aware and profound as Beckett's. If we were all like him we should all go mad, and in his youth, when he needed psychiatric help, it must have been a constant fear that his special awareness, shared by no one in his immediate family circle and only a few in the wider bohemian world that he joined when he went to Paris, could have serious consequences to his mental and physical health. The lingering vestiges of religion may also have played a part in the limbo of thinking about the world around him during the late Twenties and through the Thirties. But the growth of fascism, which brings out all the worst sides of human nature, and which he was able to observe at close quarters during the time he spent in Germany in the early Hitler years, gave him a focus

for practical action and stronger emotions. The onset
of war in 1939 could only have been a relief and it is
no surprise that he preferred France at war to Ireland
at peace. His courage, first in his Resistance *réseau*
and then in the Vaucluse where he spent most of the
war in hiding, going out with Maquis groups when the
opportunity came, is known, but has had little comment because of his extreme modesty.

Beckett's early depressions can also be connected
with his non-success as a writer until after the war. He
managed to get two works of fiction published, but they
attracted no significant attention. Otherwise his early
poetry can only be seen as a drop in the pan, while his
book on Proust came out of the difficulty that the pub-
lisher had to find *anyone* to write about Proust: Beckett
was the only candidate! Only after the surprise success
of *Waiting for Godot* and the slightly earlier acceptance
by Éditions de Minuit of his French novels was it possible for Beckett to find some escape from the deeply
pessimistic view of existence that could only make his
daily life one of constant depression. I have already
compared his life and work to that of Beethoven, a very
similar genius, who also went through periods of deep
depression and anger, from which only his work could
rescue him. Beethoven's Heiligenstadt period can be
closely compared with Beckett's pre-war and immediate post-war existence: each ended in the emergence
of new masterpieces that ushered in a revolutionary
creative period. In 1976 Beckett told me that "in old

age work must be your company", but it had long been the means by which he faced up to his deep depression as an escape. Fear of violent death never seems to have worried him during the time he was in daily danger of it during the war, but the knowledge that death does not necessarily mean immediate loss of consciousness remained with him, especially after the war, and it fuelled much of the later work.

Much has been written about Beckett's absorption in the work of Dante, certainly a major influence on all his work, principally in the strong visual element he put into many of his stage instructions and fictional writings, but also because, as with Milton, who was another major influence, it gave an imaginative background to a world after death that, if not obviously credible, could be used in an invented world of his own. Beckett's use of Christian mythology has something in common with Salman Rushdie's use of the sacred texts of Islam. There has been less objection partly because of the growth of laicism in Western Europe and partly because the complexity of novels such as *Molloy*, with all its biblical references, offers too many contradictions to the reader to enable him to make a detailed protest.

With Beckett as with Dante the horror and the black vision overwhelms whatever might be considered mildly pleasant or positive to read or look at. Dante's heaven is a pale vision compared to his hell, and Beckett's work is lightened by humour rather than pleasantness. Even the erotic episodes tend to evoke disgust rather than pleasure. Behind all of the literature of Beckett lies, like a heavy weight, his awareness of the malignity of God or nature or destiny or the Schopenhauerian "will" that underlies all movement, change or growth. One may laugh at the inanities of *Happy Days*, but Winnie's predicament quickly stifles the laughter as the horror of it becomes ever more obvious to the audience. This applies to a greater or lesser extent to all other Beckett works that briefly entertain through the humour, but soon reveal the horror that hides below.

By the end of the 1960s Beckett's work was creating new metaphors for the human condition, all showing mankind as lost in a world he only partly understood, helpless to do anything about it, like Geulincx's shipboard passenger at the very back of a boat going west when he only wants to go east. But hopeless as the world and one's existence in it may be, memory remains a potent factor in the individual's wanting to exist, and even more than that is the desire to be remembered. This comes up very clearly several times in *Godot*, and is the key to Vladimir's anger with the boy at the end of the play when he fears that the boy may not remember him in the future. The need to be remembered is even stronger than the desire to live and this occurs many times throughout the work and is also the reason that Beckett, starting with all the dead voices that Vladimir and Estragon hear in the air in Act II of the play, began to develop a series of ghosts to give a further life to the living after death.

4

Beckett's Ghosts

It is not certain that Beckett knew about the grisly experiment carried out in 1909 on two guillotined criminals, whereby their heads were put on cushions after execution and interrogated for several minutes during which they were able to respond to questions by blinking their eyelids, but it has long been known that consciousness and thought continue for some time after physical death. This means that afterlife of a sort, but not for long, does exist and many religions seem to have cognisance of this in descriptions of astral bodies and "silver cords" that take the spirit out of the body before it is delivered to some divine other place.

Joyce saw life as Purgatory of a sort, and Beckett, perhaps with Joyce in mind, developed his own concept of this in many of the later plays and some of the fiction. The ending of *Malone Dies* is where Malone's thoughts trail off into a kind of dream where Lemiel, like a demon out of Dante, goes on a killing rampage, until Malone's mind finally tapers out. *The Unnamable* also seems to take place in a kind of Purgatory that at the end dissolves with the narration in panic, suggesting that oblivion is about to follow. The middle and early later periods of Beckett's work do not yet go into the new invented theology that ends this study of his work, but it signs the way his ever-enquiring mind was about to take.

It is in *Play*, first performed in 1963, that Beckett most dramatically and disturbingly presents his vision of post-life minds continuing in a shadowy future. Three dim figures, a man, his wife and his mistress, their heads emerging from large jars, face the audience and tell their separate but intermingled stories, the complications of their relationships and the events that led up to their deaths. The story is told twice, the second time in a slightly different order and in a straightforward narrative way, but the repeat is lower in volume and the light is diminished, so that the inference is that the minds telling their separate stories are weakening and will die out eventually. This is in accordance with the known fact that the mind can continue for a while after the heart stops and physical death has been declared. The unusual stage picture startled and puzzled the audience when it was first produced, often dismissed as nonsense by conventional playgoers. The comedy of the relationships and the humour in many of the lines often brought some laughter, but gradually the horror of the predicament of the three characters began to get through, although not to the characters themselves as they go over the past events. Nor do we get more than a small hint of the causes of their deaths, which appear to be an accident in one case and suicide in another. The point is that Beckett is describing a kind of Joycean Purgatory in the three life stories and a Dantean hell in afterlife.

In other dramatic works more dead voices appear, often as ghosts, most vividly in *Footfalls*, where a woman of indeterminate age walks backwards and forwards across a narrow part of the stage, while her mother's voice hears and describes the footfalls. The mother, invisible, is presumably in bed in a room over-head, while what is seen is apparently a ghost, perhaps the daughter that was never born. Here Beckett brings up his often-repeated memory of a lecture by Jung who had talked of a child never having been properly born. The mother and daughter carry out a conversation from which it is clear that May, the daughter, who may or may not really be there, cares for her mother, either in reality or in her mother's imagination in her many old-age needs. In a final scene May, the daughter, announces the word "Sequel" and goes on to describe herself "as if she had never been" walking through a deserted church, quite invisible, again talking to her mother, who is not there, but who thinks she heard her daughter say "Amen".* The daughter, still visible to

* Beckett, *The Complete Dramatic Works*, pp. 402–403.

the audience, claims she was never there in the church and therefore could not have said "Amen". Here a ghost appears to have invented another ghost to keep the memory of an existence still alive. This is another example from Beckett of the fear of being forgotten, which first came up in *Godot* and which seems to be greater than the fear of death.

The next play that Beckett wrote was *Ghost Trio*, which, taking its title from the Beethoven composition so called, with the music accompanying the text, contains a woman's voice, very low, describing a male figure who is visible in a small room.* The man appears to be a ghost, and he casts no reflection in a mirror, although he is visible and listening to the Beethoven trio on a cassette. At the end he opens a door to reveal a small boy, his shining face expectant of his life to come, which is obviously the male figure he will be one day. The visible protagonist may well be looking at his own young self.

This later period of Beckett's writing is one of desolation, usually of whole communities in the prose works, each only a few pages long, and of individuals in the drama, where he pictures old age as lonely, often guilt-ridden and haunted by spectral presences indicating some post-life existence.

There can be little doubt that this world of dream-like reality is a replacement for lost religious belief.

---

* Beckett, *The Complete Dramatic Works*, pp. 405–14.

But the religious images are always still there in the thoughts and the words of the characters. Amy in the church (in *Footfalls*) has pity at the sight of Jesus on the cross: "his poor arm".* Beckett in his thinking moves in and out of a shadowy world, which he described to Morton Feldman as follows: "To and fro in shadow, from outer shadow to inner shadow. To and fro, between unattainable self and unattainable non-self." This becomes part of the brief text to 'neither', which Feldman, an American composer who idolized Beckett and whom the writer liked, set to music.† After the Fifties, when Beckett had achieved recognition and success and was becoming the new icon of modern literature at a time when nearly everything had been said about James Joyce and academics were looking for a major replacement, he was able to reject his self-image as a social and artistic dropout. This was the way his parents and Dublin society in general had seen him. His life had changed with success and he had now settled into a routine of writing, mostly in isolation in Ussy, sometimes spending time mostly seeing friends in Paris, or else involved in a play he had recently completed, overseeing it in rehearsal. He always claimed that at Ussy he had spent most of his time looking out of the

---

* Beckett, *The Complete Dramatic Works*, p. 402.

† The text of 'neither' reads: "to and fro in shadow from inner to outer shadow / from impenetrable self to impenetrable unself by way of neither". See Beckett, *Texts for Nothing and Other Shorter Prose 1950–1976*, p. 167.

window, but the volume of work produced, much of it reduced to only a few pages by rigorous cutting, shows that whatever time went into reflection, his productivity had not declined. And where he could not think of death and afterlife in terms of childhood devotion, he invented his own afterlife in imagination.

Religious belief in any conventional sense was now out of the question, but an emotional attachment is more difficult to reject altogether. The Bible had been the foundation stone of *Endgame*, which he still thought of as his best play, and his reading of religious texts, especially where there was a literary connection, as with Dante and Milton, continued. But he had also connected the Gnostics with Geulincx, used Manichaeism as the foundation of *Krapp's Last Tape* and followed the philosophy of Schopenhauer, who can also be connected to Geulincx, although it is doubtful that the former would have been aware of him. Schopenhauer's simple observation of the tendency of everything to grow and expand, whether it is the grass or the life of trees or the human or animal lust that lies behind the continuance of all new life, presupposed a will, but that does not necessarily suggest a conscious deity at the beginning of creation. All speculation about our existence must ultimately go back to the so-called "first cause", and Beckett in old age applied his mind increasingly – not that it had ever dropped the subject – to the possible existence of a God or some creative force that had started things happening. As for human life itself, he would often dismiss it with a shrug, suggesting that death had no importance. He had always faced it with enormous courage during his wartime days and, as an admirer of stoicism, would expect to die as one. It dismayed him when an old friend like Con Leventhal, having assumed after an operation that his cancer was over, saw it returning and died in fear and panic. I often discussed suicide with Beckett and more or less thought that he would prefer to go in that way. It might have been better if he had done so, because his long, lingering death after weeks in a coma was not a pleasant one. But ambiguity appears to have been a factor in all of Beckett's thinking and activity up to the end.

The short text of *Neither*, which Beckett eventually sent Feldman after their first meeting in Germany, depicts the speaker between two doors, neither of which will allow him entry. It is similar to the short play *Act Without Words I*, where a glass of water, held in the air above a thirsty protagonist, is always pulled back just as he tries to reach for it. Life is always holding out some desired promise and then withdrawing it. That really sums up the "Nothing to be done" that Beckett derived from Geulincx and that opens *Godot*. Beckett's outlook is directly counter to that of our commercialized consumer society where everything has to be positive and optimistic, every advertisement shows people smiling, and one is expected to reply to every greeting in a cheerful way, whatever the reality of one's situation or that of the world in general.

The final success of Beckett's work indicates the beginning of a new general acceptance of the reality of the world, probably not unconnected with the end of the age of affluence that had grown over the previous half-century during which climate change and population growth have indicated a grim future that is nearer to Beckett's world vision than that of global capitalism based on eternal optimism. The one inescapable fact that must concern everyone sooner or later is death. The shortness of life is one of the major factors underlying his work, neatly expressed in Pozzo's departing words in *Godot*: "They give birth astride of a grave. The light gleams an instant. Then it's night once more."*

Beckett's interest in the beginning of creation, whatever it might have been, has little connection with that which interests people more than God: their own survival. Beckett's evident loss of faith, or put more accurately, his loss of belief in a personal God or an afterlife – and even that cannot be said in absolute terms – carries all the ambiguities suggested by the text given to Feldman. His ghosts only seem to go on for a very short time. Now that there is a general awareness of the immensity of time and space compared to the brief span of recorded history, especially of religious history

---

* Beckett, *The Complete Dramatic Works*, p. 83.

as a blending of remembered or recorded happenings, and mythology-based traditional beliefs and dream-reality, it is difficult for established religions to impose dogma except where fundamentalism is so established that questioning is neither allowed nor present. But as science goes ever deeper into the secrets of our own and other universes, the short span of religious history and holy writ become ever more irrelevant to thinking people and today there are many writers who have not only declared their atheism, but have even advocated it as militantly as religious proselytizers have always done in the past. It is no longer dangerous in European Christian countries to be secular in one's conversation or lifestyle. Among intellectuals' atheism, and laicism in general, is so common that it is not too surprising that those interested in Samuel Beckett's work, either as general readers or as academics, view with surprise and a certain amount of hostility any detailed study of the role that religion plays in the work. It just seems too unlikely that a man of Beckett's stature in the modern intellectual world should have any firm beliefs or even a minor interest in religion at all. In the first case they may well be right, but the interest is certainly there and reinforced by his close readings of major poets among others, and they would include Bunyan, Milton and others who bring religion into their work. But the fact remains that religion is woven throughout the whole Beckett canon, sometimes satirically, sometimes as the natural conversational reactions of his characters to their situations, and sometimes as a new source of creative activity.

Another focus of Beckett's writing after the Sixties is found in works that dramatize the pointlessness of much of human activity, another way of expressing the "Nothing to be done" that is so central to his whole outlook on human destiny. In the play *Quad* four characters circulate around each other without ever touching, for no apparent reason. Various other works all describe activities of some kind as pointless, although music, especially that of the Viennese romantics, often brings some kind of near relief, often associated with dreaming, which is also a kind of ghost existence. In fact the music of Beethoven and Schubert in particular are both loaded with the same awareness of death that always haunted Beckett. It is seen in Beethoven's last quartet (Opus 135), in which "*Es muß sein!*" ("It must be!") is a grim announcement of what is coming, turning what had once been a jocular reply to a request from his amanuensis into tragedy. Lonely despair is also present in Schubert's *Die Winterreise*, a favourite Beckett work that parallels the beauty and the tragic sweetness of so much of his own art, especially the poems.

The novella *Company*, which was written at the time of Beckett's seventieth birthday, although lightened by many reminiscences of childhood, adolescence and youth, and for that reason counted among his best-known and most read works, has as its background a man lying on his back in the dark, listening to voices that in the end he recognizes all to be his own. It is an intellect buried in a void, a nothingness.

At this point in his life he could at least be sure of one thing, a lasting reputation as a major writer perhaps not yet fully understood, but certain to be read as long as literature remained an important part of the human experience. Much of his work at this time can also be seen as prescient of the coming age of austerity and growing want, and even – Lucky's speech is particularly relevant here as well as the late writings – of the end of mankind. Intellectually he would have considered that a good thing. But there is always a small hesitation in the dualism of Beckett's thinking. In *Molloy*, *The Unnamable*, *How It Is* and numerous other works including the plays, there remains a faint glimmer of hope, or a resolution to go *on*, which part of him would deny, but which remains a small but necessary part of his nature, like the small remnant of religious belief that is found in nearly all his writing. It has a strong element of defiance, against God or Nature or of existence itself. It can be compared to the very slight trace of caring humanity in the defiant last glance at the audience of the protagonist in *Catastrophe*, the most obviously political of Beckett's plays as it was written to support the Czech writer Václav Havel during his incarceration. Other last-minute second thoughts can be detected elsewhere, where his deeply seated pessimism questioned itself before disappearing.

5

From Genesis to Darwin

Beckett's view of God, although never quite defined, nor even decided, except perhaps dualistically, was closer to Schopenhauer's concept of a "will" that pushed things forward. This will, or indefinable but unstoppable force, had created all existence, although not necessarily in any conscious or intended way as seen by human minds, or even as possessing an intelligent sense. As Heraclitus said, everything is in constant flux, ever changing, ever moving on to something else. The human animal has the ability to think and to reason, although only a very few choose to do so beyond the necessities of everyday life and survival. Ambition and greed do not need the type of thinking that the best artists need, and even there the profoundest questions are often given little time. Schopenhauer's "will" has nothing in common with the God of the monotheistic religions any more than with the pagan ones. It is nearer to Geulincx, who imagines God as possibly being conscious, although not in the way that we are.

George Bernard Shaw, much influenced by Nietzsche, who declared not only that God is dead but that man would one day replace him, also uses the Bible in two of his plays, first to suggest that God is what man, through Darwinian evolution, would eventually become (in *Man and Superman*), and also that man would one day become able to prolong his life for a thousand years or more (in *Back to Methuselah*). Shaw was an eternal optimist, whereas Beckett, who knew his Shaw and came from a rather similar Irish class background, was a total pessimist, haunted by a close awareness of death and regretting that he had ever been born at all. Indeed, if Beckett's agno-atheism (to coin a word to describe his theological position) was more common, fewer couples would create new life, which would help to solve what is perhaps the single biggest problem affecting the planet because of the reproductive urge of human nature (which problem can be seen as one aspect of Schopenhauer's "will"): the overpopulation of the world. "Beckett frequently portrays parentage as crime and Nagg in *Endgame* is called an "accursed progenitor".

Implicit in Beckett's thinking is the malignity of that will. In another context this is seen as the indifference of that deity or will-nature (that makes things happen) to the reality of suffering, human and animal. From the Gnostics to much later thinkers, this malignity suggests that the deity itself is evil. God is the enemy of happiness and well-being. He would also seem to favour war over peace, hatred over friendliness and love, cruelty over kindness. This brings us back to Gnosticism and the theory that, observing the non-intervention of God to prevent or limit evil in the world, a deputy or demiurge to run the world for him had possibly been sent. The thinking of Beckett about God has involved him as far as his general reading was concerned not only in the Bible, but in all the writers who had invented a theology of their own in their literature to give a clearer idea of God and his world, and here Dante and Milton were Beckett's primary sources and inspirations. *Paradise Lost* was, as I have pointed out in *The Philosophy of Samuel Beckett*, an invitation to Beckett to create his own theology, as Milton had done.

In Milton God questions himself about his wisdom in having given man free will, which leads us over the centuries to the questioning of our existence down to the present day. The knowledge that developed out of the growth of scientific discoveries has all of it been bitterly disputed and attacked by the Christian Church, and the opposition goes on through the Enlightenment, from Darwin to Dawkins. This includes the general agnosticism of early-twentieth-century society and on to today, in Europe at least, starting from the alienation of the Christian biblical God. From this modern questioning agnosticism has become established. From the time of Luther it was inevitable that religious discord would gradually lead to scepticism. Milton depicted God being dissatisfied with man, but reluctant to destroy his own creation and uncertain that he had the power to do it. Today even religious leaders often have to admit to an element of doubt in their autobiographical writings.

Beckett took up the invitation and from the single word "revoked" in Milton's description of God questioning himself, was able to create a whole new imaginative theology, which I only touched on briefly in my earlier book.*

In the novella *Ill Seen Ill Said*, published in 1981, Beckett at the end has God making the great effort needed to destroy the world and its unsatisfactory inhabitants. In doing so he has to go back in time so that all history and all creation is wiped out, including Satan's corruption of Eve and consequently of Adam too. But hell ceases to exist when he destroys the world because there were never any sinners to send there unless it is still the home of Lucifer and his angel followers.†

But there is much more than that to this extraordinary work, because Beckett's God, whose voice is that of the narrator, is about the continuing presence on the earth, although apparently emptying itself and turning back to stone, of the Virgin Mary. She

---

*   See Calder, *Philosophy*, p. 126.

†   Samuel Beckett, *Company, Ill Seen Ill Said, Worstward Ho, Stirrings Still* (London: Faber & Faber, 2009), pp. 77–78.

is the old lady looking out of her window at Venus
and making little sorties to a grave, obviously that of
Jesus. There are twelve figures looking at her from a
distance, either the apostles or their ghosts.* If she is
alone on an empty earth, carefully watched by a God
who is anxious that his presence is not known, what
can the reason be? It can only be because the Virgin
Mary, according to general Christian belief, never
died, but was carried bodily up to heaven. The Bible
does not tell us exactly that this happened, but there
is a general view that it did, which would have been
known to Beckett. The empty or emptying earth is
very similar to that described in Lucky's long speech
in *Godot*, where it has become an abode of stones
with a few skulls left on it, or indeed the devastated
but not quite empty landscape described in 'Lessness'
where some disaster, perhaps a nuclear war, has taken
place. Or it may even be the French town of Saint-Lô,
destroyed by Allied bombs during the Normandy land-
ings, as described by Beckett in a piece entitled 'The
Capital of the Ruins'.†

Only when God has accomplished his great task of
wiping out the earth and all his creation, including
to his obvious regret the Virgin Mary, probably his
most favoured person as she is totally without sin,

---

* Beckett, *Company, Ill Seen Ill Said, Worstward Ho, Stirrings Still*,
pp. 45–50.
† See *As No Other Dare Fail: For Samuel Beckett on his Eightieth
Birthday* (London: Calder Publications, 1986), pp. 71–76.

and probably also the last survivor, does God "know happiness", which are the last words of the novella.

What Beckett has done is finish Genesis and also the New Testament. The audacity of this invented theology is incredible and, although very short, of the same order as Milton's theological creation in *Paradise Lost* and *Paradise Regained*.

Beckett's narrating God is anxious to hide himself, and the author was obviously reluctant for this masterpiece, which James Knowlson describes in his biography *Damned to Fame* as a "meticulously woven tapestry of words", to become too well understood.* It is obvious that Beckett did not reveal many secrets from the very late works to Knowlson, and on the only occasion when I discussed *Ill Seen Ill Said* with the author, he was not pleased that I had discovered what I had. Perhaps one reason for his reticence was that he never wanted to face the attacks of organized religion and of the faithful generally. At the time of his appearance as a witness in the Gogarty trial, his complete honesty about the Christian faith and his indecision about it led to his being pilloried in the Dublin newspapers, to the great distress of his mother in particular, and the memory was probably still painful. He knew how sensitive religious discussion can be among those of different faiths or none, and it was natural for him to avoid argument that could only lead to embarrassment or worse.

---

* James Knowlson, *Damned to Fame: The Life of Samuel Beckett* (London: Bloomsbury, 1996), p. 668.

But when a writer takes it on himself to invent and put on paper the voice of God, he in a sense becomes that God himself. And it must be said that the old woman, who we now know is the Virgin Mary, is very similar to the old lady who rocks herself to death in *Rockaby*. But she is also obviously, but not completely, based on the figure of his own mother who, when he returned to Ireland to look after her, was dying. It must have occurred to him then if not earlier that her name May is almost Mary. Certain things remained linked in Beckett's mind. The death of his mother is associated with his play *Krapp's Last Tape*, where "the vision, at last", as described earlier, is recorded on the tape. He knew that his departure from a strict faith had been very painful to her, so that guilt must have played a part, both in the written work with its bringing together of filial devotion and speculation on matters of religion, death and human destiny, and in his depictions, on stage and in fiction, of the world of the Bible and of the life he observed around him.

Anyone who has had a strict religious upbringing can never get the emotional and nostalgic need for it entirely out of the system, whatever the intellectual conviction that the whole thing is impossible mythology, unbelievable to any thinking mind. The need to protect the faith of a mother who could only view his own doubts with great pain and whose need to believe that heaven would follow death, which was now so imminent, was a clear obligation. Inevitably the need to

be able to think independently himself while support-
ing his mother in her faith meant that Samuel Beckett
had to be mentally in constant flux between his own
agno-atheism and his mother's biblical faith. In invent-
ing the voice of God watching over an old lady years
later, he was only echoing his own earlier position.

In the work that followed *Ill Seen*, namely the
novella *Worstward Ho*, the same voice might well
be present, but the tone is different. It is a voice
questioning itself at every moment. It is a description of life coming into being, and before that the
beginning of creation much as science views it, with
the slow coming together of different elements in
time and space until the impossible happens and life
starts, and a being is there that can finally stand and
become intelligent. It is not clear whether this is the
first creation, but the probability is that it is, and
God is not mentioned, nor is it clear whose voice is
urging everything "on". If my supposition is wrong,
then God, having destroyed everything in *Ill Seen
Ill Said*, has done it all over again. But in any case
the language is so different that it is unlikely to be
a sequel in time to Beckett's previous novella. One
reason to support this view is that *Ill Seen* can only
take place long after the crucifixion and from the Old
Testament down to the present, whereas the creation of the world is, although undated in *Worstward
Ho*, obviously meant to cover an immense period of
time, many billions of years. Nor is there any given

ending. The narrative goes into an infinity of space and time into the cosmos.

Worstward Ho is much quoted for its famous passage about failure: "Ever tried. Ever failed. No matter. Try again. Fail again. Fail better."* This is usually taken as another piece of comfort for those who are unambitious or whose plans go wrong, another plank in the platform that Beckett has built over the years to demonstrate the futility of success. Other writings, notably the second *Act Without Words*, in which two men on alternate days share the same suit and whose days are either lacklustrely dreary or full of activity, all carry the same message. In Beckett's dialogues with Georges Duthuit, speaking of art in general, he says: "To be an artist is to fail as no other dare fail, that failure is his world," and even the *"Fallor, ergo sum!"* of the early poem 'Whoroscope' is an example of this.†
But Beckett's characters in general are all failures, from Murphy through Molloy and Moran to even the very late protagonists. Life is short and must end, and death is the final failure that makes nonsense of being born and living. Failure ultimately belongs to God, however he is defined. His creation is pointless except as the presence of eternal and unending growth, but in spite of regeneration all growth appears to carry its own

---

* Beckett, *Company, Ill Seen Ill Said, Worstward Ho, Stirrings Still*, p. 81.

† See: Samuel Beckett, *Proust: And Three Dialogues with Georges Duthuit* (London: Calder Publications, 1965), p. 125; Beckett, *Selected Poems 1930–1989*, p. 6.

destruction within itself, so that nothing is permanent. The new replaces the old.

This would appear to concur with Schopenhauer's view, although he never directly says so. The "will", as seen by Schopenhauer, is an indefinable force that drives things on and makes them happen. Free will, according to Genesis, was given to man by God, but Adam betrayed him and his eternal punishment has to be endured by all his descendants, that is to say mankind, as a result. Jesus was meant to rescue us from that curse, but quite evidently he has failed to do so. All this, of course, means nothing to the average churchgoer, who, however much he might read the Bible – and few do – never thinks out the logic or consequence of what is related there.

It is interesting to contrast Schopenhauer's concept of the "will" with that of Geulincx, because both had a profound effect on Beckett's thinking. The will of man, according to Geulincx, can be compared to that of a man on a boat travelling west who wants to go east. It is the will of God that drives the boat in his chosen direction. Man's will can only take him as far as the back of the boat, which all the time is travelling in the other direction, unless he wants what God wants, but even then he can, when he gets to the front, only become the priest or the acolyte of God, which is what the faithful do.

Both in his writing and in his notes on the margins of what he was reading, Beckett refers several times to Geulincx's boat, even bringing in Odysseus from Homer, who in a different context had to cope with the will of Homer's gods, except that in Greek mythology man sometimes had a better chance than with monotheism, which is really always absolute.

Beckett's early reading and studies had a greater influence on his late work than on the writing until 1960, partly because he had by then escaped the influence of Joyce who exhaustively looked at everyday life to bring out its complexities and to parallel modernity with antiquity, and partly because an old mind compulsively has a tendency to go back to early memories. In creating his own theology he was using the dogmas established in an age when people believed in miracles and supernatural happenings as a matter of course. But the tone here is very different from that of the *Molloy* trilogy, which dealt with established religion in a satirical and mocking way, bringing out the many absurdities. In *Ill Seen Ill Said* he is making sense of the dogmas in a manner devoid of his earlier humour. He has in a sense become the same author as that of Genesis.

Whereas Joyce retold Homer's second epic in *Ulysses*, adding many inventions of his own, Dante had expanded the extremely vague medieval concept of what the three worlds of afterlife might be like in *The Divine Comedy*. Milton built a whole epic around the pre-Creation war in heaven to explain the presence of Satan, who leads his army of dissident angels against God. So did Beckett do something as daring in *Ill Seen*.

But the outcry from the faithful that would follow a revealing of the meaning of the text, especially in his native Ireland, made it necessary for the author to hide the story he is telling well away from the general reader, while leaving enough clues for it to be discovered later.

As a result even James Knowlson, his principal biographer, could only comment that it is a beautiful piece of fine prose, making no effort to discover its meaning, and John Fletcher, who had already written much about Beckett, including a well-produced bibliography with Raymond Federman,* has nothing to say about it or any of the other late prose fiction, except that they cannot be rated with the work of the immediate post-war period, which will always be considered Beckett's major work.

This illustrates which I said earlier about the similarity between Beethoven and Beckett and their three periods. The general incomprehension that for so long cloaked the composer's late works can likewise be applied to the writer. Even Beethoven's most ardent admirers felt that advancing years and his deafness had ushered in a musical dementia, so that he was producing unmusical sounds that had no sense for ears that had welcomed the great middle-period symphonies, the opera *Fidelio* and other works contemporary with them. *Ill Seen Ill Said* is not just the voice of God

---

* Raymond Federman and John Fletcher, *Samuel Beckett: His Works and His Critics: An Essay in Bibliography* (Berkeley, CA: University of California Press, 1970).

speaking carefully, hiding his presence and who he is from the reader, but it is also the voice of Beckett, hiding behind his creation in a language that is full of biblical references and very rich, so musical that when read aloud its beauty evokes wonder, but the secret of the old woman is hidden just the same. When I spoke to him about it, having just discovered this one important part of the secret – the presence of the Virgin Mary – he was not pleased, pleading loss of memory, but he knew I was right. Three words in the text, which had not struck me with their full significance earlier, told me that the old woman had to be the BVM from the New Testament. It was in Milton that the inspiration for the full work was revealed, and I have explained this in my book on Beckett's philosophy. Other meanings came out later, but only after other dogmas had come to mind.

The first give-away of *Ill Seen* is the phrase "full of grace", the second of the Hail Mary prayer, known to every Catholic from the time of first being able to learn it.* It is carefully planted, certain to be discovered one day, as it was by me, but only after knowing the whole text well for some years and from having organized many public readings. The Milton reference had to be seen sooner or later, but not too many academics

---

* "At last in a twin movement full of grace she slowly raises the bowl toward her lip while at the same time with equal slowness bowing her head to join it." Beckett, *Company, Ill Seen Ill Said, Worstward Ho, Stirrings Still*, p. 62.

interested in the great writers of the twentieth century ever go back to earlier classics that they probably read once years ago and see no reason to return to. Other than that, biblical knowledge is needed, but also the various dogmas that have grown over the course of Christian history, often from a papal statement or that of a theological figure who was influential in his time. The bodily ascension of Mary is not in the Gospels, but has become a tenet of much Christian belief. At any rate it is certainly the reason the Virgin is still around, observed by God, when the world seems to be coming to its end, and it must be because she is without sin and God's favourite being that the ascension is still delayed in the novella. This too is ambiguous because she occasionally disappears, so that it might well be her ghost that is "ill seen".

What cannot be missed are the references to the crucifixion and to the apostles, or indeed to the grave that the old lady visits.

Whether it is still the voice of God that one hears in *Worstward Ho* is debatable. But the tone is so different, and the cautious "carefuls" of the earlier text are not there, so I think not. What Beckett has done is invent a voice that seems more abstract than that of the God of Genesis, nearer to Schopenhauer's "will", if that could be imagined as a voice. Man has always thought of God in human terms, so that God is man-like, but with greater intelligence, a kind of giant figure some-where out of sight, once believed to be up in the sky where heaven was situated. The realization, first that the earth is not flat but round, then that the stars are other suns or constellations, and finally that we are not the centre of all things but a tiny unit in an immense amount of space, has made conventional faith in the Christian view of existence no longer credible except to the most fundamentalist mind that ignores scientific discovery and denies everything that makes nonsense of its pre-Enlightenment view of the world.

Worstward Ho is as close to a description of how existence started, and from it life itself, as is possible in literary terms. Some force (as in Schopenhauer's "will") drives things "on", so that by the accidental collision of one thing with another the impossible finally happens and the two things become one. Eventually, after an immense amount of time and an immense number of things that do not meet, something does meet and meets something else until finally life exists. We are looking at near infinity.

But the moment comes when life exists and then finally human life.

"It stands. What? Yes, Say it stands. Had to up in the end and stand."* Throughout this extraordinary text the impossible becomes the inevitable. Life comes into being, then human life, then intelligent human life, increasingly learning to understand its environment and the universe or universes that surround it. This is

---

* Beckett, *Company, Ill Seen Ill Said, Worstward Ho, Stirrings Still*, p. 82.

the will at work, but in no way is the will described as benevolent. Existence exists so that pain may exist. Pain and suffering and inevitable death: there is nothing benevolent, good or desirable in this. The distant thinking of the Gnostics emerges in Beckett's work, and the deep influence of Geulincx becomes ever clearer. If late Beckett, like late Beethoven, is treated as fine work but of little consequence in the canon, it is mainly for three reasons. The first is the difficulty most readers have in connecting with Beckett's profoundly pessimistic view of life and all existence, so contrary to our commerce-driven consumerist society where optimism is forced on us against all the evidence. The second is the extreme economy of language that he has forged to carry the content, which can be too difficult for the conventional reader who does not want to delve too deeply into what appears at first glance to be a forbidding text. The third is the fact that Beckett's writing constantly throws up highly quotable phrases and innovations of language that carry a message of their own that can easily be read in a very different context.

So, for instance, the text can be seen to be about failure. This it is in a way, but it is a theological failure or a cosmic one, where the responsibility falls back on the will. Beckett has often in the past held up failure as a human characteristic that carries no blame, which is a comfort to those without ambition or any desire to advance in life. "Ever tried. Ever failed. No matter. Try again. Fail again. Fail better." This is often taken as a half-serious statement relevant to some small upset, whereas the author intends it to refer to the whole of existence. Creation, growth and advance in terms of progress is not a positive thing but a disaster. Even Darwin did not perceive any benevolence in evolution, but only the continual advance of power. In economic terms capitalism exactly fits the description, and greed, which is the motivating force behind power, although looked at with a negative eye by much of civilized society, is certainly responsible for much of the suffering that pervades the world.

As well as a very accurate description of creation and evolution, *Worstward Ho* carries the inevitable message that everything is for the worst, and existence is inherently evil. Hence the title *Worstward*. And the final words, "Nohow on", carry the same message.* There should be no progress because it is itself evil. The "on", which is usually taken for an injunction not to give up, is also evil, because the "on" only leads to more evil.

To sum up, these two late works of Samuel Beckett occupy the same place in his opus that the late quartets do in Beethoven's, and rather than being politely dismissed as they usually are, should be considered as perhaps his most significant and important work. They deal with the reality of human destiny, life on earth and its meaning, but also explain how that life came

---

* Beckett, *Company, Ill Seen Ill Said, Worstward Ho, Stirrings Still*, p. 103.

about. He has entered the world of science as well as that of imaginative literature and theology. The latter, continuing from his early contacts with religion, was transformed by his genius into both a parody of the Pentateuch and a finishing of it. In the final paragraph of *Worstward Ho*, Beckett shows us the unfortunate but possible human future: man invading the stars, moving out to other universes, which could be a Shavian hopeful concept. But Beckett would hope not.

6

Existence and Defiance

All of Samuel Beckett's work can be seen as a search for meaning, starting with his fiction where he was trying to discover who he was, why he was so different from his parents and their comfortable, self-assured bourgeois lives, and then having to make sense about the world around him. He certainly understood the nationalistic and religious conflicts of the Ireland in which he grew up, moving towards the independence that it achieved in 1922 when he was sixteen and still at Portora in the Protestant north, whereas his home and family were becoming part of a minority in the largely Catholic south, although the moneyed classes still controlled their privileged status amid continuing violence and a civil war that affected them hardly at all. There is little to show that Beckett had much interest in the political events that were going on around him, but he must have been aware of them. On the other hand the difference in religious conviction must have preyed actively on his mind during those teenage years and by the time he left the north the probability is that he was well on the way to a questioning agnosticism.

The presence of religious dogmas is portrayed by him often with sardonic humour, or as the everyday thoughts and speculations of his invented characters, and sometimes as central to a narrative that paralleled the scriptures, and gradually in the many shorter prose works from the 1960s onwards they became metaphors. They showed humanity in situations of dire distress or, as in the short story 'The Lost Ones', published in 1970, engaged in pointless activities while trying to understand the world they inhabited. The quest for meaning is always there because in the last analysis that is what every writer of importance is seeking. But in Beckett's case it is always a picture of humanity trapped in a hostile environment from which it is struggling to escape, but cannot.

Sometimes it is described as a mind enclosed in a confined space, a metaphor of the thinking organ inside the skull. In the short prose piece 'Imagination Dead Imagine' from 1965 that enclosed mind is hurtling through space, as we are all travelling through space on the planet earth, and this is prescient of *Worstward Ho* with its vision of man invading the cosmos. In *Murphy* a whole chapter describes Murphy's mind! "Murphy's mind pictured itself as a large hollow sphere, hermetically closed to the universe without." The author brings in the Buddhist concept of nirvana, which is what

Murphy is seeking, the peace of nonexistence, but on the way to that was the world of contemplation which was Beckett's own. "But how much more pleasant was the sensation of being a missile without provenance or target, caught up in a tumult of non-Newtonian motion."* The journey into space is a vision of human evolutionary progress that Shaw and Nietzsche would have recognized, but the mind, which wants to understand what is outside its prison, remains trapped.

All of Beckett's thinking in a way is an attempt to get outside the world of ignorance that encloses us. For centuries it was the Christian Church that entrapped the mind, stopping enquiry through dogma. The Reformation gradually loosened that authority, followed by the wars of religion and then the Enlightenment, until today agnosticism and atheism are common among those who have escaped organized religion and the ever-powerful and long-lasting emotional pull of early childhood religious observance. The Muslim world, although split doctrinally between the Sunni and Shia factions, as well as other sects, has never undergone a reformation, and where doubt of what is taught exists, it is usually found wiser to be silent. The Eastern religions are in general more tolerant and allow discussion and disagreement, which is also the case with much of Judaism. But as politics gets mixed up with religion there is a tendency to go

---

* Samuel Beckett, *Murphy* (London: Faber & Faber, 2009), pp. 69, 72.

backwards and fundamentalism returns, bringing with it intolerant cruelty and tribal hatred.

Beckett's vision of a world that encloses thought and thereby limits discovery is therefore very relevant to our troubled age where speed of physical communication does not necessarily include the flow of ideas. The minor wars that constantly break out across the planet are mostly tribal, but religious conflict is itself tribal, and everywhere the thinking, non-doctrinaire minority has to censor itself and be careful where it expresses its thoughts.

Beckett's metaphor of entrapment, whether of the individual mind or a section of society itself, is therefore very relevant. Escape into a world of wider knowledge and free thought is always difficult and the individual must proceed with caution. There is a tribal need to conform but a mind that has the courage to free itself from the world of dogmas and conventional opinion with all the taboos and restrictions that different societies and cultures impose as a matter of course is rare and often in considerable danger from those who hold firm to a faith or an opinion.

That is why Beckett has so often to cloak his thoughtful investigations into the nature of things, the existence of God, the meaning of our existence and, at bottom, of human nature itself in secrecy, using metaphor and, very often, the stories that have grown around and through Christianity itself to create fictions and dramatic situations that can appeal to audiences through the highly original and musical nature of the writing without giving away their significant meanings that would often be unacceptable.

Our knowledge of the world we inhabit has grown largely through scientific discovery, assisted by the invention of printing, which enabled new knowledge to spread rapidly. The biggest entrapment of the enquiring mind is the shortness of life itself, and the increasingly commercialized nature of a culture that tries to get the young interested in ephemera, fashion and celebrity, something that obviously limits the number of intellectuals interested in any serious enquiry into meaning. Although the growth of electronic media would seem to offer an expansion of human knowledge, its intellectual impact has been small, partly because the ability to concentrate the mind is reduced by a multitude of trivial distractions and partly because it is increasingly difficult to study a phenomenon as a whole, rather than as a series of fragments. Isolated bits of knowledge gathered through the Internet cannot be put into an organized history, and it is so much easier to plagiarize than to produce an original document that real scholarship for its own sake must become ever rarer.

The enclosure of the enquiring mind in a small space is a constant theme in Samuel Beckett's vision of the world. It is the hindrance that nature, in our present state of evolution, and the limitations of the unenquiring human mind together put in the way of our knowing more about the universe we inhabit, and knowledge in general. 'The Lost Ones' is a powerful metaphor in which the known world is enclosed in a cylinder, covered by a roof in which some believe there may be a trapdoor opening the way to what is above. The cylinder covers an immense space in which its inhabitants wander aimlessly about; the ambitious and curious ones queue up to climb ladders set against the wall, while others sit listlessly against the sides of the cylinder. The ladders are of different lengths, some with extensions, nearly all of them with several missing rungs, unevenly spaced, so that climbing up is a great problem. The ladders all lead to holes in the walls, some giving a bare shelter to the climbers, some with tunnels that may run into other tunnels, but that may just stop, making return difficult. Many theories abound, especially of what might lie outside the cylinder. Perhaps the tunnels or some of them might eventually lead to the world outside and the open air! It would be hard to think of a better metaphor for the human condition on this planet, although today, with the opening out of space through immense and powerful telescopes, we are getting to know more and more about outer space, and through microscopic investigation into the inner space inside the atom. It would increasingly seem probable that existence is infinite up and down, outside and inside. Time too seems infinite. We can conceive of there never being an ending, but only recently has the thought occurred to a few that there may never have been a beginning. And if space is circular, what lies outside that circle?

The contents of time and space are more central to Beckett's writing or thinking and conception of the world than to that of any other writer except perhaps pure scientific literature, except where, if Beckett can be seen as a philosopher, he can be described as an imaginative scientific researcher as well. Where, as in 'Lessness', his metaphor describes an open space rather than an enclosed one, it is a scene of devastation. In that short work there are six survivors of a catastrophe, six members of a tribe that has been devastated by some act of God, who is cursed for it. It may have been created by an act of man, a nuclear bomb for example, but in that world of believers God would nevertheless carry the ultimate responsibility.

Beckett's disdain of human activity, vividly described in 'The Lost Ones', is brought out many times in his work. We rush around in different activities, all of them ultimately pointless, because they must end in illness, failure, death or all three. The only benevolent activity and it was very much his own, is kindness and a helping hand. No one was ever as generous as he was and it is his only positive message on how to get through life. Godot will never come, but until the arrival of death, which will certainly come, there is not only "time to grow old" but time to share, to offer, to show sympathy and to comfort. In the words of Vladimir:

Let us do something, while we have the chance!
It is not every day that we are needed. Not
indeed that we personally are needed. Others
would meet the case equally well, if not better.
To all mankind they were addressed, those cries
for help still ringing in our ears! But at this
place, at this moment of time, all mankind is
us, whether we like it or not. Let us make the
most of it, before it is too late! Let us represent
worthily for once the foul brood to which a
cruel fate consigned us!*

Throughout Beckett's work there is a growing conviction, not too obvious and not much noticed by his
many admirers, that the dichotomy between nature
and whatever one associates with nature, including
a conscious God or a Schopenhauerian "will", is an
oppositional confrontation between that side of the
human understanding and intelligence that we see as
benevolent, generous and compassionate, which at
bottom is the creative will of the artist, and the basically selfish and greedy nature of most of humanity,
which cannot escape its tribal background. This side
of human nature is akin to that of other feral animals
that live in packs, always at war with other packs: in
other words spiritual man as opposed to tribal man. In
my previous book on Beckett I referred to spirituality as

---

* Beckett, *The Complete Dramatic Works*, p. 74.

being a quality to be found in a few rare humans, not in any form of divinity, which is basically only interested in growth and increase, itself a negative and probably evil presence. There is already more than a hint of this in Beckett's dialogues with Georges Duthuit, which define the spirituality of the artist as deeply rooted in failure, because the artist must always see himself as a failure, his ultimate vision always a little nearer, but never quite reachable. Evil will always triumph, although there have been good periods when for a short time the philosophical and the artistic mind has temporarily broken through to create a short time of civilized and benevolent existence: the Greece of Pericles, certain moments of the Italian Renaissance, periods of the nineteenth century when culture and scientific, philosophical and political thought had moments of breakthrough, and when even peace took over society for a while, at least in some places. But such happy periods were always short, and the worst of human nature, power lust, tribal hatred, greed and the opportunity to dominate, would quickly return.

The First World War, when Samuel Beckett was still a child, brought to an end an age when the prospects for a brighter future seemed to be on the horizon. The rapidly mounting death toll of wartime casualties brought that Shavian optimism to an end. Calvinism, with its preoccupation with predestination and hell-fire, would have troubled Beckett from his schooldays, and his discovery as a mature student of philosophical dissent from the orthodoxy he had grown up with was to shape his thinking from then on. Rather than dismiss religion, he was to use it as a tool to turn it on its head, finally depicting mankind as the victim of a savage and hateful force or destiny that the established religions called God or Allah or Jehovah, if they saw that force as conscious. Otherwise it could only be seen as a distant and indefinable presence which had only the function to create, if there was an original creation, but otherwise to promote ever more growth. Capitalism as an economic system is about the growth of wealth and while socialism has the same purpose there is the basic difference of how that economic growth is divided and whom it benefits. Beckett always avoided political discussion except in private and there his sympathies were always on the humanitarian left. His charitable instincts could be compared to that of the Jesus of the Gospels and while he had nothing against Marx, with whom on most issues he would have agreed, he knew perfectly well that the worst of the human instinct would always create inequalities. He was even tolerant of greed up to a point in individuals, because when he was earning considerable sums through royalties, and even more when he had a large amount at his disposal from the Nobel Prize, which he won in 1969, he let it be known that he was willing to help anyone who came forward – he had other writers mostly in mind – and he gave what was asked, however unreasonable the amount requested.

At the same time he realized that generosity cannot be for the whole world. One can help a few, but not everyone. He knew that socialism as an ideal might be possible occasionally, but that corruption and individual greed and the lust for power would sooner or later bring back inequality and injustice, and that has of course always happened. His understanding of human nature enabled him to be tolerant of dishonesty and minor rogues, and some with whom he associated, including some in the theatre, he helped with money when asked, as well as helping, usually anonymously, poor students who confided their problems to him.

His various metaphors to describe the human condition, such as those mentioned above, are not limited to groups or societies, but often individuals as well. In the short story 'Ping' he is looking at someone who might be a helpless prisoner with "all white bare white body fixed one yard legs joined like sewn". The body can see the white space around as if it were a prison cell, and can occasionally hear a "ping" sound. He can wonder about his environment, but not understand it. He has obviously been there a long time, and the white light and the heat come and go. "Ping of old only just perhaps a meaning a nature one second almost never blue and white in the wind that much memory henceforth never." But the end is near and it comes: "old ping last murmur one second perhaps not alone eye unlustrous black and white half closed long lashes imploring ping silence ping over."[*]

It is a description of the end of life and as a metaphor it can be seen in many contexts, that of a solitary prisoner in a cell, an invalid dying alone or a torture victim, but without question it is about death and "ping" is the final sound of life. What it brings to mind is another Beckett text, the play *Catastrophe*. This depicts a man slowly being turned into an immobile statue, a work of art. The character known as the Director, like a film director in a studio, gives orders to an assistant how to arrange the figure as he wants him to look, while the audience watch. The man makes no effort to resist as he is gradually changed from a human being into an object, supposedly without feelings or even any awareness of what it happening to him.

The play was a response to the Czech Communist regime's imprisonment of Václav Havel, one of the country's major writers. Although Beckett had always refused to make political gestures, unlike most other writers living in France, his objection to censorship, especially in his native Ireland, was well known and on this occasion he did respond with a directly political play which in its meaning and impact could hardly be bettered. The man is dehumanized without the smallest gesture of protest, until the moment when the Director declares that what he is looking at is perfect. Then, at

---

[*]   Beckett, *Texts for Nothing and Other Shorter Prose 1950–1976*, pp. 123–25.

the last moment before the lights go off, he raises his head and his eyes looking at the audience express a vivid defiance.* Beckett's victims usually suffer without any gesture or sign of more than a stoic awareness of what is happening to them. It is God or human destiny or some terrible circumstance that brings human life to an end, perhaps only with a "ping". Usually that death is only near, sometimes it is in the past, remembered by ghosts or voices that prolonged life after physical death. But here, in this remarkable play, Beckett becomes almost the Shavian optimist, at least in so far as he depicts a last act of human protest at the malignity of all authority.

Catastrophe can be seen in narrow political terms, or else as a metaphor for man's eternal struggle with everything that holds him down to a few brief years of life on a remote planet, circling a sun that is part of an immensity of space that we are only beginning to understand a little, now that the human mind has developed enough to throw off the restrictions that authority, including the organized religions, had imposed on the enquiring mind. That spark of defiance in the protagonist's eye is the last ray of hope that Beckett leaves us to offer an alternative to the bleak hopelessness that characterizes most of his work. It is only a gleam, but some will consider it better than nothing.

---

*   Beckett, *The Complete Dramatic Works*, p. 462.

7

Spirituality and Genius

Spirituality is perhaps best defined through its opposite. We can all recognize the human nature that has no time for ideas, culture, aesthetics, knowledge for its own sake and in general any thought that it is not aimed at a specific goal or advantage to the individual involved. Spirituality stands outside the personality. It can be seen as an instinct towards goodness, like Adam Smith's "hidden hand", a ray of benevolence that like a virus takes hold of the mind and looks at the feral side of human nature – indeed of all nature – with horror and that has the courage to stand firm when faced with the tyranny and the authority of power that wants to go in the opposite direction.

Spirituality is often confused or associated with religion and this is not necessarily wrong where a certain number of individuals are concerned, some of whom are considered to be saints. But it certainly does not belong to religion in so far as authority is concerned;

all organized religions are about maintaining an established status quo and are intolerant to whatever resists that authority. Christianity, before the Emperor Constantine called the Council of Nicaea, consisted of many different sects, all looking for answers to questions that were still being formed, and like Judaism, Buddhism and Hinduism it allowed for argument, disagreement and investigative discussion. But the Council ended all that. Like Islam, Christianity has always enforced unquestioning belief and obedience to orthodox teaching. Many other Christian groups then existing, such as the Arians, as well as other gospels, were declared to be heretical at Nicaea and expelled, while over the centuries those that considered or wished to return to an agnosticism or an earlier doctrine such as Manichaeism were cruelly punished.

Spirituality is characterized by free-floating thought that can make discoveries by observation, accident, instinct or teaching, and its relationship to genius can be traced, but not properly defined. I have mentioned Beethoven and his three periods. The first was developed out of observation and teaching as he followed what he knew from the work of Mozart, working within an established tradition, that of producing a rich and melodic series of sounds that were aimed to please a particular audience, one that would subsidize his career. Mozart advanced that tradition to new heights and the indications are that had he lived longer, rather than dying at thirty-seven, he might have become a Beethoven. Certainly the revolutionary element was there in his genius, and time and maturity would almost certainly have brought out the movement into another sphere of music. There are already sounds that predict middle-period Beethoven in the *Requiem* and even passages of *The Magic Flute*.

It is in fact through art that we best discover spirituality, although some, and here I think in particular of Bertrand Russell, might find it in mathematics, and certainly, observing the wonders revealed by science, that might have a strong claim. I mentioned accident and instinct and, in the case of Beethoven, his deafness, which did not enable his ears to hear what was going through his mind, may have contributed to the quantum leap from the great symphonies and chamber music of his middle period to the late quartets: these were found incomprehensible to their early listeners, but are regarded today without reserve as art of the highest spirituality and genius. The mind made a jump from what were already works of genius that had become understood into another sphere of even greater spirituality. The spirituality is a constant quality that lies behind the genius, which then becomes a form of creation. In other words spirituality is the spur, and genius the accomplishment.

Is the human mind here paralleling a force of nature? The evolution of species and of the thinking mind have obviously much in common. It is the presence of accident in all the meetings and non-meetings that eventually become a presence that is significant. This Beckett described accurately enough in *Worstward Ho*, delineated in the last chapter. The difference between the creating mind and creating nature would seem to be the absence of spirituality in the latter, whereas it is obviously present in the former. The difference lies in the purpose of the two. I have been defining human creativeness as spiritual and therefore benevolent, whereas the creativity of nature, always without any awareness of consequence, and redolent of suffering, misery and both natural and human cruelty, is malevolent and therefore evil. The Gnostics recognized evil, thought it could not come from God, who was ignorant and possibly unaware of the plight of humanity, and therefore they blamed it all on a demiurge, an inept deputy whom they saw as probably being the devil.

The Cathars of Provence, probably the most important Manichaean sect known to history, could not quite bring themselves to believe that the Christian God they worshipped could really be evil, but they developed a highly puritanical society in which every step was taken to combat the presence and influence of the Devil, who obviously played a larger part in human affairs than any deity, benevolent or not. Evil was held at bay by rules, principles and a lifestyle that excluded all pleasure from life, and they thought in absolutes. Their courage when cruelly persecuted and destroyed was legendary. The extreme limits on their thinking would have excluded the spirituality that I have tried to define here. The Christianity that destroyed them was both corrupt and hypocritical with a papacy and a clergy that were materialistic and self-deluding enough to think that a society such as the one they controlled in no way excluded them from heavenly delights in the future. God had to obey a papal decree, because the papal word was absolute. But spirituality would soon be there in the great artworks of the Renaissance, which was the positive result of the fall of Constantinople and of other world events that would soon revive the culture that died with the end of the Roman Empire.

In following the growth of great painting, first in Italy, then in the Netherlands, Germany and France, we see spirituality growing in visual terms, as genius developed out of it, and slowly the other arts followed. The freedom to think independent thoughts, not regulated and controlled by the confessional chamber, if one had the ability to keep those thoughts to oneself, gradually grew out of the creative process, although efforts were made to contain that freedom, the most terrible of which was to be the so-called "Holy" Inquisition, which turned the confessional into a public trial and spectacle. Nevertheless, the enquiring mind, once it had discovered itself, could not be wholly stopped, because the creative process, starting with a few whose talent was dependent on the ability to observe and consequently to challenge, thereby opened the doors to genius. This was seen in the works of such great artists as Leonardo da Vinci and Michelangelo, but also in the thinking of such logical philosophers as Giordano Bruno, who was eventually burnt at the stake for his views. Bruno, following Copernicus, perceived the vastness of the known world, both the universe or universes around us and the possibilities of endless space within the atom. He nevertheless saw God as the uniting factor in a transcendental universal system where everything was part of everything else. This was too radical a concept for the simplistic minds of the Church authorities to stomach. All speculation held the danger of being heretical. When Giambattista Vico picked up many ideas from Bruno he was careful not to name his sources. Beckett became acquainted with Bruno and Vico while doing research for Joyce, although he may have known of them earlier. But their recognition of the creative nature of the mind of the artist and of the growth of thinking capacity in general, with the spreading of new knowledge derived from developing science, and in particular Vico's new historical interpretations of events,* during the period of the High Renaissance was to lead to the recognition of genius as something different in kind from talent, craftsmanship and exceptional ability. Creative talent had from the earliest times been something to be bought or at least recognized through payment or some other mark of recognition, such as the conferment of rank. Farinelli, the famous castrato, was made in effect

---

* See Calder, *Philosophy*, pp. 104–105.

prime minister of Spain by the king who had brought him there to sooth his melancholia and to sing to him every night before he went to sleep. Mozart, who had felt deeply the humiliation of having to sit with the lower servants at the Archbishop of Salzburg's table, was one of the last creative geniuses to be so treated in the Austria of his time, once that genius had been recognized. Beethoven, born only fourteen years later, had even the Emperor's brother, the Archduke, who was his piano pupil, treat him with the respect due to a social equal and an artistic superior. Genius came to be recognized and throughout the nineteenth century not only in music, literature and painting, but also in philosophical, scientific and political thinking, as an aristocracy of the creative intellect. Unfortunately, with the growth of commercial pressure, much of this new status for the creative mind has degenerated into a cult of celebrity, so that much artistic activity, often with no training or superior guidance behind it, has become conceptual in the sense that the artwork in question was purely a figment of the artist's mind, needing no particular skill, only an objectivized idea.

It is impossible to generalize about non-representational modern art, because some of it is a return to primitivism from an established tradition, as with Picasso, some merely the charlatanism of those with little talent who claim that art is whatever they choose to call art and some with a personal vision where mysticism, coupled with a form of dream reality and some industrial imagery caught in the brain, all combine to make a new creation that might be visual, auditory or an idea that can be put into words or some symbolic form. At any rate, the many dualisms about art from the beginning of modernism – 1906 seems a good date to start with, although many would put the date earlier, in the Impressionist rather than the expressionist area – is a good analogy for the dualism of religion. There is the conflict between form and content, which in art is the difference between classical and romantic models, and in religion between good and evil, which in pre-Christian thinking and even among Gnostic thought is often seen as a masculine-feminine division, with the masculine representing the more primal and naturalistic – that is to say animal – side of human nature, and the feminine the more humane, civilized, artistic and even spiritual side. In scientific terms that dualism can be represented, like DNA, as two strands that coil around each other so that between them something occurs, the creation either of life or of art or of a new idea that leads to a progress of evolution.

The dualism about the nature of God is constant in the history of all religions even going back to the oldest, Zoroastrianism, and becomes polytheistic in the paganism of the Greeks and Romans. The perception of evil in the world is obvious even to non-human life, and early Christianity, in which we must include the Gnostics, was dualistically Manichaean. But the orthodoxy established at the Council of Nicaea did not trust any thought or belief outside what was preached as dogma. The power of evil, rooted in nature and in the human personality itself, would also attract support, and therefore it was downgraded to an alternative picture of a simple God always being kind and good, which is the image given to young children that tends to last for life. The presence of a demiurge, too powerful to be contemplated by the Church militant, and too often associated with the Devil, has therefore to be denied, although the belief went on lingering for a long time among those Christians who were willing to think and discuss these things, but not too obviously.

The search for meaning is a purely human search: other forms of animal life accept the day-to-day search for food and rest, and when threatened the need is primarily for survival. Age wears down the body, which becomes gradually weaker and then dies, although most certainly an instinct warns the animal when the end is near. Only the human, usually from sometime in childhood, is always aware of mortality and the certainty of death, and the concept of religion, however much disguised by preaching the love of God for mankind, has basically only one purpose: to assure the individual that he or she will survive in another and possibly better life. This is however questioned by many thinkers, inside and outside the many faiths of mankind, and in the case of Beckett, the conclusions of Arnold Geulincx were those that led him to the premise that he most closely identified himself with, namely that God is too far away even to know or in any way to care about our existence or happiness. The prospect of an afterlife disappears with the concept of a missing God, however defined, although in the absence of any belief there still remained for many a vestige of the childhood hope of something that the logical mind could not totally accept. Even the most acute and intelligent consciousness must be aware of its fallibility. What finally emerges, and this is clear from Beckett's subtexts, is an attitude of defiance, not only against the idea of the God one was taught to believe in as a child, but even more so at all the injustices that poison the human condition, primarily the injustice of being a speck of nothing in the endless immensity of infinity, and then all the injustices that the human species invent to make not just life but existence itself intolerable, except on a day-to-day or hour-to-hour basis for certain individuals at certain times when some circumstance offers a temporary relief.

The intention of this chapter is to define spirituality and genius, which affect time and space as little else does. In the progress of human evolution, so vividly described by Beckett in *Worstward Ho*, both play a role. Spirituality is obviously very different from everything we associate with materialism, either the effort to survive on the most primitive level, or the ambition to succeed in the hunt for power, wealth or importance of some kind. It is self-denying as seen by those who want what our society is designed to make them want and can only be understood by a mind that by instinct or example is looking for a peace based on understanding. People have gone to lonely places to contemplate and the more mystical religions, not the organized monotheistic ones, are relevant here, but the art world with its fixation on an aesthetic that only the individual creative mind can understand and recognize, is easier to penetrate. Spirituality depends on instinct allied to reasoning and it offers an escape from diurnal banality, but only for a while. It is a factor in genius, which can only be recognized by what it has produced after that production exists. Music offers the best examples, at least to me, and the sounds produced by the late works of Beethoven, and in a different context by Schubert, open a world of spirituality that is pure genius.

There are many things that the untutored lay mind cannot understand but knows to exist, such as the way sounds and pictures can travel through space to be caught by a radio, mobile telephone or screen. In the same way thoughts seem to be able to travel from one mind to another by some process of telepathy, not necessarily by any act of will, but by some process where the same thought goes simultaneously into two different minds. Perhaps one day it will be discovered that dreams are also transferable by some process that is not yet understood. Our understanding of the non-material world will obviously continue to grow unless, as has happened in the past, authority, in a less open society, shuts down scientific discovery. Although spiritualism has declined in general acceptance and belief, it is not that long since many who rejected organized religion still believed that it was possible to communicate with the dead through a medium or in some other way to reach the minds of the dead. Although the ghosts invented by Beckett as a device in his later plays and some of the fictional writings are literature, there always remains the possibility that his extreme agnosticism could have contained, if not actually a belief, a lingering desire for some kind of existence to continue after physical death.

Genius obviously applies to all human discovery and it can have a practical purpose. The early cave paintings depicting animal life were made possible, not just by the desire to reproduce a facsimile of what had been observed, but by the need to study the animals so that they could be captured for food. Paintings produced for a patron to collect had the same purpose: payment would buy the means to live. Philosophy either created rules for the state by explaining meaning and what was needed, or else it offered knowledge to those who sought it. And the arts have the double purpose of teaching what the lay person could not discover alone and of giving pleasure. When the most basic needs of the body, food, shelter and sleep, have been met, the next human need is entertainment. This of course comes at different levels, and the class system, which no society has ever been able to do without, offers different levels of entertainment to different levels of intellect and understanding.

The genius that applies to a Darwin is obviously different from that which applies to an Einstein and different again from that which we think of in connection with Adam Smith, John Stuart Mill or Karl Marx. None of these apply to Shakespeare, Rembrandt or Beethoven, whose struggles to find what they were looking for are different from the genius of Mozart, to whom writing music was as easy as breathing.

Spirituality would seem to be in the personality as an innate quality that develops with time and that is related to genius, which, however, grows through experience and instinct into something indefinable until it is recognized, although sometimes it is not.

In the case of Samuel Beckett, whose growth as an artist and thinker I have tried to follow in my book on his philosophy, and here in his pondering on the existence of a God or creative force, one can say that starting as a searcher for meaning as part of his decision to be a writer, he had first of all to find a style that could carry the meaning that came to him through reading, research and the natural spirituality of his personality, and then to use his knowledge of the time he had come through – Irish parochialism, Nazi terror, the occupation of France and his crises with health, despair and a deep sense of failure – to realize the full potential of the genius that was there all the time. The search for God could only lead him to a deep void, so he invented what he could not discover, except as an incomprehensible concept, namely something close to Schopenhauer's "will", which was a new, invented theology of his own, in which he became the mouthpiece of the evil creator of a cruel and undesirable world that he then attempted to destroy, and of a vision of evolution moving through eternity that he could only call "worstward".

8

Protest and Defiance: The Human Factor

All of Beckett's writing makes it clear that tragedy is the human lot, that all relief is short-lived and in no way a part of human destiny, which is simply to be a link in the chain of creation and evolution. Shakespeare's vision was nearly identical, even in his comedies, as in Jaques's famous speech defining the seven ages of man. George Bernard Shaw saw almost as deeply into human destiny as did Beckett, but he paid no heed to the plight of the individual. Unlike Beckett he had no lingering emotional attachment to religion. The shortness of life for one person or one generation was of no consequence to him. What mattered was the continuance of evolution; man's destiny lay in the distant future when he would become godlike in the sense that he would resemble man's early concept of God and become more powerful and also live for perhaps thousands of years, as the Old Testament suggests he once did, an idea on which Shaw's play *Back* to *Methuselah* is based. Also man would develop many of the other powers that used to be attributed to God. He takes his idea largely from Nietzsche, but extends it.

I have already pointed out that Beckett considered Shaw's concept of the human future, which is perhaps fairly typical of the post-Darwinian intellectual thinkers of the nineteenth century, and put it into the second part of Lucky's speech in *Waiting for Godot*, but he emphatically denied it was the probable future in the third part, and saw a negative future for humanity instead. The probable human history of the future looked black enough when Shaw died in 1950 and he had long stopped looking ahead. The Second World War was over then, but the threat posed by the existence of nuclear weapons was very real, and that threat is even more ominous today with world conflicts as often based on religious fanaticism as nationalist or racial convictions. But Shaw was by nature an optimist with great self-confidence and no religious belief to make him regret a possible afterlife, and that nature carried a non-self-regarding stoicism that the more sensitive and faithless Beckett could not share. Beckett lost his faith logically, but not emotionally. What is implanted in childhood can never be totally lost. Shaw, like Beckett, made use of biblical mythology in his work, but only to predict a future superman who would be godlike.

Beckett's pessimism gave him a reflective, melancholy life, relieved by human contact with a large number of friends, many of whom never knew each other, but in convivial company he could relax and escape the abyss which he knew was never far away. Life is always characterized by pain and the best solution is to find ways of diminishing it. But the defiance of the whole injustice of the known world and our consciousness of it is, if not an answer or a solution, still remains the last possible human response, useless perhaps, but the most human reaction left to us. It is the act of the heretic, of the rebel, of the nonconformist, of the outsider. It means putting oneself outside the traditional idea of the creation by God or Nature, or even of accepting many of the mores of conventional society if one perceives an injustice or hypocrisy. Beckett did this most effectively in his play *Catastrophe* with the single glance of a defiant eye at the audience before the lights go off. Defiance is the last act of humankind against the whole injustice of its existence.

Defiance is the positive display or act of protest. There is protest in all of Beckett's work, implicit in the early period, blatant in the *Texts for Nothing* and the *Molloy* trilogy, and even in the quietist late work; the *Texts for Nothing* are protests, not yet quite defiance. A lone voice speaks in a wilderness of loss, unable to go on, yet having to. Rejected, getting lost and weaker, facing the realities that it realizes were always lies, and in one of the author's most moving and telling phrases: "the same lie lyingly denied, whose the screaming silence of no's knife in yes's wound, it wonders".* There are thirteen *Texts for Nothing*, always a significant number for Beckett.

Defiance is often present in art, especially when, *in extremis*, the artist rails at the destiny or the nature that he sees as his mortal enemy. Beethoven's last gesture when dying, and a thunderstorm broke out, was to rise in his bed and shake his fist at the lightning that flooded the room, crying out "*Plaudite, amici, comedia finita est*" ("Applaud, my friends, the comedy is finished"). Beckett's last words are unfortunately unknown; his last written words are found in two short poems that accept the inevitable death that he knew was near, and a text, 'what is the word', written in his two main languages, that expresses the helplessness of a failing mind to find the words to express a thought, and yet at the end, aware of its own folly in dementia and unable to overcome it, he is still able to express that inability in a cadence of great beauty:

> folly for to need to seem to glimpse afaint afar away over there
>
> what –
>
> what –
>
> what is the word†

---

* 'Texts for Nothing XIII', in Beckett, *Texts for Nothing and Other Shorter Prose 1950–1976*, p. 53.

† Beckett, *Selected Poems 1930–1989*, p. 117.

Perhaps the nearness of death creates its own defence against fear and the capacity to defy, let alone to protest.

The defiance of the gods goes back to Greek mythology. Prometheus defied the gods by stealing fire from Olympus and bringing it to mankind, which can be compared to the Gnostics' search for knowledge against a Christian Church that either wanted to confine learning to the priesthood as a way to keep power or saw it in biblical terms as coming from the Devil, or as in Genesis with the corruption of Eve and Adam. The Roman Catholic Church has always opposed allowing the laity to read the Bible, knowing that its many contradictions and anomalies would confuse simple minds and raise doubts. Although most Protestant sects encourage Bible reading, it is doubtful if many readers understand it well enough to be able to do anything other than quote particular passages, and copies left in hotels by the Gideons usually have selected passages indicated to fit particular problems or moods. On the whole organized religion wants congregations to acquire only such knowledge as is advocated from the pulpit. "All you need is faith" is the adage most often used. But faith, which I once overheard defined in a conversation by two young clerics in a restaurant next to Exeter Cathedral as "active trust", requires or indicates an inability or an unwillingness to ask questions. Questions are what organized religion dislikes most and discourages from early childhood by dogma learnt by rote, often in the form of prayers that frequently start with the words "I believe". It was questions that started the Enlightenment of the late-seventeenth and eighteenth centuries. Reason, after all, is what separates humanity from other forms of animal life, and it is our ability to reason that makes all free thought possible and that in itself is what leads to questioning.

Much lip service is paid in Western civilization to the desirability of democracy as a form of government. It can however be argued that not all societies want or trust democracy, which can so easily become corrupt, and which really only works according to its theory where the right to vote applies to a society of a high educational standard, and where that society shares an ethic and a sameness of outlook whatever the class or ethnic divisions happen to be. This does not often happen in practice. Differences in religion are one of the main factors here, but there are many others such as those involving tribal and cultural ethnicity, appearance and economic circumstances. A high level of education is the principal answer to overcoming the differences and divisions in society that can lead to a workable democratic system, but this is little in evidence except in small enclaves and a few small, mainly northern countries, and even there population movements are diminishing the tolerance necessary to achieve true democracy and an intellectually free and open society.

The Enlightenment was seen by the established Churches as their biggest threat and enemy, so that the only way to re-establish their authority was to reduce the capacity to reason and with it the ability to question. The return of fundamentalism in the form of the Tea Party and other neo-conservative movements in the United States, the revival of extreme right-wing, nationalist and racialist ideologies in Europe, the ever-continuing tribal conflicts of Africa, together with the antagonisms of Arabs and Israelis, of Hindu India and the Islamic Asian world, and other confrontations across the planet, all point to a disintegrating world, overpopulated, unequal and likely to self-destruct. Politicians are of a lower calibre everywhere than in the past and altruism is almost unknown.

This would have been of no surprise to Samuel Beckett, who in his work predicted in different ways the future that is becoming the present. The return of fundamentalism, much of it based on religion, some on nationalism or tribalism, coming at a time when the blunders of politicians, often as corrupt as they are stupid, and the greed and wild gambles of the global financial world, all combine to make any recovery impossible, and is a return to primitivism and the revival of the worst in human nature. Greek civilization declined with Rome, although some learning continued. But Christianity stopped that, and it took a thousand years before the Renaissance revived a culture that led by degrees to the Enlightenment. The nineteenth century had great minds that made great discoveries, above all a return to philosophical thinking. Although society was very restricted as far as most human appetites were concerned, and much hypocrisy became endemic, it was still an age when the mind triumphed over the censorship of thought. As the Victorian age came to its end, there was a general optimism about the future and a better society seemed certain. That confidence in a possible utopia is best reflected in the work of George Bernard Shaw, a religious unbeliever who cared little for the fate of the individual compared to what he saw as coming for the human race, well on its way to a good and cultured society where human happiness would be within the reach of all. The First World War put a stop to that and all the disasters, cruelties and horrors that followed were a direct result. As the twenty-first century progresses, in spite of the weak promises and predictions of politicians and most journalistic commentators, the future can only be worse. Small wars will turn into big ones and the weapons of mass destruction that have been held back for so long are certain to be used by someone. Deterrence is no longer a valid argument. The willingness of so many fanatics, spurred on by a faith to welcome martyrdom, can only lead sooner or later to a world war that may destroy all life on our planet.

Samuel Beckett, great humanist that he was, did not see such an outcome as a disaster. If there is no God that cares for us and no afterworld ready to receive us – only the possible presence of Geulincx's distant, uncaring, indefinable creating force, or Schopenhauer's equally indefinable but observable activity – then it would be better to end all the suffering that is inevitable in human and animal life and bring the whole human adventure to an end. Our planet can then go on among all the millions of others in outer space in an infinity that will never end and may never have begun.

9

The Meaning of Nothingness

Those who wrote to Samuel Beckett asking him to explain the meaning of some of his work often received a reply saying that the closest explanation he could give lay in a quotation from Democritus: "Naught is more real than nothing". In a way, Beckett is echoing the last lines of Macbeth's great speech defining life before he goes into his final battle: "a tale told by an idiot, signifying nothing".

Almost certainly the origin of Beckett's philosophical nullity lies largely in his discovery of Geulincx with his emphasis on the need to be humble before the greatness of God, who might however be so far away that he is unaware of our existence – indeed also of the existence of the planet on which so many of us are tiny insignificant creatures living short lives in the timelessness of infinity. The nature of that God can never be discovered, but he or it, however defined, certainly has no resemblance to anything human as most religions have always claimed. As Baudelaire put it: "God is the only being who, in order to reign, does not even have to exist".* Nothing can ever be proved about God, nor even defined, although for centuries many minds have endeavoured to do so and many mythologies have become the background material of religions, both organized and privately invented, many of which have become faiths designed to protect authority, give comfort, reduce fear or reassure those facing death.

Beckett's own fictional theology in his late work is a brilliant literary creation, but it must not be taken to denote faith. Richard Ellmann, taking a phrase from Joyce, described Beckett as "the Nayman of Noland",† which the author could hardly have disputed. The origins of that perception of nullity in human existence must go back to his first doubts at the injustices of Calvinism, although it only became a conscious conviction predicting his future about the time of his mother's death, carefully crafted as the "vision at last" in *Krapp's Last Tape*. It was a time when he was back in Dublin after the war to comfort her at the end – not easy, as at the time she must have been trying to get him back on the road to faith, and he would not have said anything to give her more pain at such a time. But caring for his dying mother also gave him time to reflect on his own position as an unsuccessful writer, unsure of where he wanted to go intellectually, still not

---

* Baudelaire, *Fusées*.
† See *As No Other Dare Fail*, p. 79.

sure of his own talent and tortured by thoughts of the religion he had abandoned, while hiding this as far as he could from his mother who was confident that an afterlife awaited her.

The realization that his future lay not in avoiding his black view of human destiny and the meaning of life – quite apart from general thoughts about the existence of God – but in using that dark vision to underpin the writing he wanted to do, was the decisive point in his career that would ultimately enable his genius to be recognized. The tenets of religions other than Christianity were already well known to him, and Buddhism in particular contributed much to *Murphy*, his last pre-war novel. *Watt*, written mainly during his years in hiding in Roussillon, made much use of biblical material, but also expressed his awareness of the cruelty and destructiveness of human nature, as an important part of God's nature, in the episode where his narrator feeds young rats to their larger parents as well as other animals, saying "it was on these occasions, we agreed, after an exchange of views, that we came nearest to God".[*]

Beckett's nullity is based at bottom on his protest at the apparent malevolence of God or Nature, and although he does not directly identify the two, as Geulincx and his contemporary Spinoza do, the suggestion is always there, as it is in the other philosopher

---

[*]   Samuel Beckett, *Watt* (London: Faber & Faber, 2009), p. 133.

he most admired, Arthur Schopenhauer. It is a nullity based on dualism, not only on the black-and-white dualism of Manichaeism and the Gnostics, as well as earlier religions, but also on his own position between an inability to accept the religious beliefs in which he had been brought up and the lingering emotional attachment to the same. But like many who have been accused of heresy or atheism by the co-religionists of their time, and I refer especially to the latter day Cartesians like Malebranche, Geulincx and Spinoza, Beckett's mind went on enquiring into the beginnings of existence, and the nature of God and of human destiny. His pessimism and awareness of the immensity of pain and suffering in the world would have been even greater had he lived into the twenty-first century where the return of many fundamentalisms, brutal conflicts and corrupt and misguided governments would lead to economic crises that have only just begun and are certain to get worse, provoking ever more misery. At the same time, natural disasters are increasing as an overpopulated planet is rapidly running out of water, food, energy and other things that make life possible.

Agnosticism in no way reduces the need of the questioning mind to go on thinking about the great cosmic unknown. Faith has no need to question, and is probably held back by fear of what it might discover. The courage of such thinkers as Geulincx is even more extraordinary when one realizes that he, and other philosophers who delved into the same speculations, paid no attention to human happiness, which they saw as a delusion based on selfishness that was incompatible with the humility that alone might attract the favour of God.

But this humility again puts God into the category of a tyrant and, as I have pointed out in *The Philosophy of Samuel Beckett*, as a tyrant who can always be compared to an earthly ruler, a king or a dictator to whom one must pay homage and obey. Not only can such a world authority be seen as evil, although there are altruistic exceptions, but so can a divine presence, whether viewed as a supreme power or a demiurge. Beckett obviously inclined towards seeing all ultimate authorities, singular or plural, as malign. And the only human answer to which he inclined was protest, which in some of the works at least, becomes defiance.

With the Second World War over, Beckett was able to return to creative writing, and soon he was producing those middle-period works on which his reputation chiefly depends. They all proclaim defiance, contrasting the comfortable bourgeois world in which he grew up with that which he discovered through poverty, observation and his wartime experiences. God is there in the background, but not as something to be admired or loved, but as the cause of all suffering or as being indifferent to it. Above all he satirized it, bringing out his whole battery of intellectual wit and sardonic humour. But all the work dramatized the individual's struggles to survive in a hostile world. The ever-present malignity, whether of nature or of man or of God, always showed the hopelessness of hope itself and the inevitability of death, however long delayed; Vladimir and Estragon struggle on, having no choice, to survive a little longer, but Godot never comes. His existence is only confirmed by the boy (or boys) who arrive. The boy may well be a metaphor for all those who proclaim the existence of a God whom we can never see. Vladimir's sudden rage at the boy, who cannot remember having seen him before, has a double meaning: he is afraid that he will not be remembered by the boy in the future – the only evidence that he had once been there and is not forgotten – but also that his presence will, he hopes, be reported to Godot, who at that moment at least represents God.

Perhaps the last comfort to Samuel Beckett in old age could have been the realization that he himself would be remembered, because his work was already so well known that it would long survive him. The hope, or the belief, that one will survive in an afterlife is of course the basis of faith for nearly everyone, but not for Geulincx, who does not even mention it. His whole emphasis on humility and the unquestioning acceptance of God's will brings human existence down to the same nullity that governs Beckett's thinking. There is no reason to believe, if God is possibly unaware of our very existence, that there is anywhere for us to go. We are of no importance at all in the great scheme of things and death must be final. The inference is that Geulincx accepts his non-being without protest. The will of God is final.

Beckett is often called an existentialist, and he is very close to that definition, but not quite. The "perhaps" that he used as a key word in his doubts and general thinking presupposes not just an agnosticism but an a-agnosticism that the real existentialists such as Jean-Paul Sartre did not share. Sartre talked of "being and nothingness" and accepted absolutely the inevitability of total extinction. Beckett was perhaps ninety-nine per cent on the way there, but the "perhaps" remained in his mind. The lingering nostalgia of childhood indoctrination was certainly one factor, but there may have been others. At least, when asked if he was an atheist, he always gave a reluctant and half-believable "No". This did not mean that he saw any concept of heaven after his demise. Like Geulincx he saw the possibility of a far-away divinity, indefinable except as a will, but outside any human understanding. I have described Beckett in the past as a stoic. The Stoics had learnt to live with uncertainty and were willing or had the courage to face whatever was coming. This is also certainly true of Beckett.

Stoicism is an attitude, not an answer. It is not incompatible with the occasionalism of Geulincx, which is an attempt to define causal relations. In philosophy this is seen not as a natural phenomenon, but as the intervention of God's will, which neither

Geulincx nor Schopenhauer attempted to define, except to the latter it is Nature itself which moves things for no particular motivation that can be observed, so that even Schopenhauer could be defined as an occasionalist.

Where does this leave Beckett? His ethics are very clear, combining Geulincx's humility with a generosity that in social terms meant a willingness to share what he had and what he earned with anyone who needed help, and with many who did not need it in any meaningful way. It involved him in putting himself out in any way he could to help others. When confined to a solitary room in the old people's home where he finally collapsed, aside from giving author's copies of sometimes very luxurious and expensive editions of his writings to anyone who passed by, it consisted of feeding the birds outside.

All his work was in a sense a search for the God in which he did not believe except as a remote and indefinable possible presence, as well as a protest against the injustices that cover the planet with pain and misery and the creation of a self-created literary theology. He also gives us, as a final autobiographical effort, several pictures of an old writer at the end of his tether, still able to create something beautiful, moving and true.* He had already in a simple poem, an addendum to his novel *Watt*, described

---

*   *Stirrings Still.*

himself and the nullity that runs through all his work as follows:

> who may tell the tale
> of the old man?
> weigh absence in a scale?
> mete want with a span?
> the sum assess
> of the world's woes?
> nothingness
> in words enclose?*

---

* Beckett, *Watt*, p. 215.